Whe  Don't Quit

Reflections of a part-time winner

Dear Helena,
Stay Lucky!
Neell

ISBN: 978-1-6958-0611-5

When Losers Don't Quit

Reflections of a part-time winner

Neill Johnstone

Preface

Prizewinning – it sounds like a great hobby, doesn't it? Push the magic button; fill your boots with goodies; repeat. Well, I hate to break it to you: there's no magic button. And, for a lot of the time, there's a distinct lack of goodies. The simple fact is that, as with any discipline, it takes time and it takes practice. Yes, there are highs; but there are also lows.

I've won cologne from Paul Smith and cologne from Peperami (yes, it does smells like a bit of an animal); gorgeous fitted shirts from a Kensington outfitter and a shapeless red hoodie from an online smut pedlar; I've won tickets to watch Norwich City draw, and tickets to watch them lose. But mostly, I win nothing at all.

Don't get me wrong – I get my share, but you can't win them all. More to the point, you can't even enter them all.

For the last few years I've spent a lot of time thinking about this hobby, better known as comping. I've thought about what I like and what I don't, and why; the various ways my friends would judge me if only they knew how I've debased myself to score cheese, and whether it's really true that nothing whispers 'amour' like the scintillating scent of spicy sausage.

Not all of these thoughts have been worth having, but such is my curse. I used to be smart – I've got actual certificates about actual stuff. However, the prolonged campaign of shock and awe to which my offspring have subjected me has taken its toll. To paraphrase Douglas Adams, the first few years of contesting the same arguments on a daily basis were the worst. As for the next few years, they were the worst too. The next few years of arguing I didn't enjoy at all, and after that I went into a bit of a decline. Indeed, these days I can barely operate a spoon.

To be sure, there are worse forms of mental trauma. But if sleep is the brother of death, then I'm pretty sure parenting is the cousin of PTSD. For my part, it reduced my beautiful mind into bubble and squeak – a riot of vignettes with no clear beginning, middle or end.

What to do then? Languish in the intellectual rubble, or, as folks smarter than I have suggested, seek to better understand my life by putting a narrative frame around it?

Whether transcribing one's life really can result in enlightenment I couldn't say. What I do know, however, is that in my case, writing brings me, if not inner peace, then at least an opportunity to formulate thoughts away from my cacophonous munchkins and their incessant cluster-bombing of my delicate synapses.

Thus, the book you hold before you represents my best effort to extract some kind of sense from the heap of noodle inside my noggin. It started out as an A–Z on the subject, but my mind wandered. Perhaps inevitably, my linear intentions went all lateral and my gentle meander got waylaid with digressions increasingly tangential.

So, a book of facts, this isn't. Neither is it a how-to guide. If you want to pigeonhole it, it's a memoir. More specifically, it's an introduction to the pleasures and frustrations familiar to those in the comping community. It also provides an insight into how this hobby can affect mental wellbeing – both positively and negatively. Think of it as an open-top bus tour through the scenic world of prizewinning, piloted by a bewildered tweed albatross.

I'm hopeful this book will make you think, if only a little. Failing that, I hope you at least manage to see it through to the end – it's worth it for the speedboat chase.

Antidepressants

Romantic, isn't it, the idea of packing it all in and moving back to where you first met, so you can settle down, buy a house and raise a family?

Romantic, or possibly impulsive. But when you can't see any way that you'll ever afford a home near where you work, and you don't actually like the place that much anyway, it seems like a reasonable option.

So, if one of you has a job that is not only transferrable, but in real terms will earn more in a city you both love, that ticket sells itself, right? Your soon-to-be ex-colleagues have promised to chuck some freelance work your way, to tide you over while you find a new job – life is sweet!

Nine years later, however, that new job still hasn't materialised, and the clients you've built up are increasingly taking the freelance work offshore. You've no family or friends in the area, so your every day is silent and lonely. Evening time, your other half works, so you barely see them either. Existential crisis ensues.

This midlife malaise sooner or later happens to everyone. And everyone has the same genius solution: have a baby.

It's this kind of rational decision-making that separates us from the animals.

The same kind of rational decision-making that after three years of thinking life has never been so damned hard and thankless, concludes that what's needed – what's *really* needed – is a second mewling, puking time-vacuum.

It's not that I regret having children. I just thought I'd be better at parenting. Then again, I wasn't expecting my precociously over-achieving first-born to have reached an adolescent level of belligerence by the time he was seven. Meanwhile, as my youngest continues to scream in my face when I put him on the toilet, the life-affirming aspects of parenting are less closely spaced than I'd hoped.

So where do the competitions fit into this? Validation.

When it comes to giving positive feedback on your performance as a parent, children are notoriously tight. Indeed, nothing in my life has made me feel more of a failure than parenting. As for work, the best praise I can hope for is that my last remaining client can't keep his head above water long enough to action the inevitable offshoring of my livelihood.

This stands in stark contrast to comping, where people who don't know me from Adam call me up or e-mail me just to say 'Hey! You! The winner over there!' My kids don't do that. My friends don't do that. And I certainly can't imagine ever having a job where my boss would do that. It's validation that civilian life just doesn't offer. And yep, you bet I appreciate the love.

There doesn't even have to be a prize – that validation, that love is there for the taking, as I found when one-time Children's Laureate, Michael Rosen retweeted a poem I wrote for a National Poetry Day competition. Sometimes, affirmation like that is the only sparkle in a day of drudge.

But drudge in itself I can handle. Extended periods of isolation, those I can handle too – there's something to be said for the novelty of being able to hear your own thoughts instead of the constant shrieking, fighting, yelling and door-slamming that come with my children. Honestly, I've seen cage fights held with more decorum.

What is difficult is that as a parent, you're only as happy as your unhappiest child – and my first-born's happiness is transient at best. After a while, this starts to take its toll on your mental health.

The funny thing is, I never considered myself to have low mood, never mind depression. That was before my mum shoved the following list of symptoms into my hand:

- difficulty concentrating, remembering details;
- fatigue and decreased energy;
- feelings of guilt, worthlessness, and/or helplessness;
- feelings of hopelessness and/or pessimism;
- sleeping problems;
- irritability, restlessness;
- loss of interest in activities or hobbies;
- persistent sad, anxious, or 'empty' feelings.

To my mind, these all came with the territory of parenthood; nevertheless, I had to accept that when people start lobbing breadcrumbs at you on account of your waddle and twaddle, it's time to seek help.

Cutting a long story short, I committed to a programme of counselling, cognitive behavioural therapy and mindfulness, rounded out with anti-depressants. So if you want to know why I've come to crave those moments of joy so badly, there's a clue.

My dad always said never to judge a man till you've walked a mile in his moccasins. Academically speaking, that's a great philosophy; in practice, however, it can be problematic. In my case, it's not that I don't value empathy, but rather that my mum has always forbidden me from borrowing other people's shoes due to the untold damage it might do my feet. And as I'd hate for anyone to suffer a bunion on my account, I'll simply confess that when I'm in a stinking funk, the rush of endorphins when I win can sometimes do more for me than the prize itself. In other words, I use prizewinning as a crutch for my mental health; that it happens to come with a souvenir is a fantastic bonus.

Of course, not everyone is quite so enthusiastic about the analgesic properties of comping. Every so often I stumble across an ill-informed promoter who thinks it's OK to ban compers from their giveaways – a policy that's not only in breach of Advertising Standards Agency guidelines, but which makes as much sense as banning jockeys from the St Leger Stakes. Sometimes, these misinformed souls even try to tar the whole community with broad-brush accusations about compers entering any old comp for any old tat. I say, screw that, I really needed that toothpick.

OK, so that last bit's a porkie – I've never tried to win any quantity of toothpicks – but I will admit that when I first started comping, I followed the common rookie path of favouring competition quantity over competition quality. Naturally, it wasn't long before the prizes didn't start rolling in and I decided to change tack.

But comping for any old tat? Don't be daft. Obviously, some promotions are more exciting than others – we'd all rather win an iPad than a pint glass – but if it's neither use nor ornament, who's going to waste time trying to win it? Besides, who's to say what constitutes tat? Speaking as someone who has literally Freecycled dirt, I know for a fact that one man's muck is another man's most-wanted.

To take another example, bagging an eight-foot bust of Jeremy Clarkson is not my idea of hitting the jackpot. Still, that doesn't stop me being happy for the lad who did win said statue as he's given his parents' front garden a real focal point. Moreover, he's also found a unique way to bring the residents of Salford closer together.

At the same time, I'm also sufficiently familiar with addiction to recognise compulsive behaviour on my own part. To this end I will come clean: I had no immediate need of the Popeye cap I won the other year, but given the 50/50 odds, I couldn't resist the punt. In short, I am what I am, and that's all that I am.

Confession, they say, is the road to healing, so I hope you won't judge me too harshly. In any case, I suspect I'm not the only person who has, at some point in their life, entered a giveaway more for the hit than the prize – after all, who doesn't want to be a winner?

And yet, for all comping is about making people happy, it isn't a sexy hobby. There – I've said it. Sega isn't making a videogame franchise for compers; her majesty won't be knighting anyone for being really good at it; and the BBC is more likely to replace Strictly with public flogging than Britain's Got Compers.

The sad truth is that among the civilian population, there is little admiration for the gentle art of comping. Some folks are sniffy, others are just plain baffled ('you win things … as a hobby?').

I conducted a quick straw poll of my Facebook friends to gauge their opinions on the matter. I got two responses: a positive comment from a fellow comper, and a like – from my mum.

Based on that convenience sample then, I'm assuming at best that my friends find comping about as interesting as my personal sleep schedule; or at worst, are so cheesed off with Facebook polluting their newsfeed with the tedious details of my leisure time that they've muted me already.

A lack of enthusiasm I can live with. More disheartening, however, are the pooh-poohers – the people who laugh at compers and insist that competitions are a waste of time as no one ever wins them.

Notwithstanding the fact that belittling people for enjoying themselves is the lowest form of bullying, the suggestion is plainly fallacious, as a brief review of the facts will testify. I keep a spreadsheet of wins on my phone for just such an occasion. A conversation about a recent or impressive win doesn't hurt either – whether I win big or win small, either way, I'm a winner.

And it's not just prizes that make a winner – it's attitude too. What's the one thing that repeat winners share? Determination. Whether you call it perseverance or plain stubbornness, no one gets through the first couple of months without it. I can't begin to imagine how many thousands of competitions I've failed to win. But trifles are trifles and should be treated as such. If I can handle a quiet week, I can certainly dismiss a doubting Thomas.

'You're just lucky – I never win anything.'

I tell you what … I'll see your old chestnut and raise you another, because the harder I work, the luckier I get.

To be sure, there'll never be Olympic medals for comping. But if there's one thing this hobby has in common with the innumerable sporting disciplines out there, it's that if you want to win, you've got to train the right muscles – in this case, your luck muscles.

I've heard folks put negative attitudes down to jealousy. But, as my old man used to say, never attribute to malice that which can be put down to ignorance. It's amazing how many mockers and gloom-mongers button up once they're on the end of a bumper birthday gift or an extraordinary little treat. You see, winning feels good, but sharing that good fortune and making other people happy too? That feels incredible.

Bookies

The FIFA World Cup used to be the cornerstone of my life. I got together with my other half during the 1998 tournament, and exactly four years later, we were married. Another four years on and we were still gorging on as many matches as we could fit around full-time work. Come 2010, however, our first-born was three months old and did not care for international football – not one little bit.

I was on the afternoon shift at that point, but every time I sat down, he'd wail. Watching Germany dissect England is excruciating at best, but there's nothing like doing it while you slow dance with a mardy bairn to really put the boot in. It was at this point that I stopped watching football.

That's not to say I stopped taking an interest, however, as I'd just learned about matched betting – the clever-dick form of gambling where you don't end up out of pocket as the bookies pony up the stakes for you. This was about the same time as the bookies discovered social media. They gave away so many free bets that, for a few months, I had a nice little side hustle. By no means did I make a fortune, but I did make sufficient money from one company that I was barred for being – quite literally – a liability, and taking more money out of the company than I was putting in.

This was especially disappointing as these guys ran loads more competitions than any of the other bookies, with the result that, on top of the free bets, I'd also won branded hoodies, poker chips, playing cards and a polo shirt. Plainly, I was having a ball (a rugby ball, to be precise).

The merchandise was great, but there was icing on the cake too: I accumulated £180 of credit at a store specialising in soccer apparel, both modern and retro. This explains how I ended up with, among other things, an Atlanta Chiefs jersey that is every bit as flammable as its 1981 counterpart and an exquisite replica of Zaire's 1974 World Cup strip that I'm no longer able to wear since becoming a biscuit shovelling snack beaver (yes, I do blame the children).

The credit came in the form of gift vouchers, so it was a case of use it or lose it. And being the sort of person who wouldn't buy so much as a cheese straw without first checking in to Quidco, there was no way I was going to fill my basket with big stuff and then let the chump change slip through my fingers.

Goodness knows how long I spent trawling through the bin-ends, with spreadsheet and calculator to hand, but eventually I found a beautifully coloured Paraguay scarf and a couple of keyrings to round out the order. I possibly had to write off as much as seven pence worth of prize money, but somehow I summoned the inner strength to stomach such egregious waste.

Keyrings, of course, are both subtle and useful, and mine began to earn their keep almost as soon as my prize parcel arrived. Football scarves, by contrast, are bluntly ostentatious statements of tribal identity, and – when they deviate from the designated colour scheme – arguably iffy in one-horse towns.

That's not to say that the fine citizens of Norwich would have given me a good pitchforking had I openly allied myself with Paraguay, but I was nonetheless unsure whether wearing foreign football apparel would have been cricket. To this end, it sank to the bottom of the winter accessories box, where it lay, cruelly neglected, for the next few years, until the fashion pages of the *Guardian* informed me that football scarves were back in vogue – for that week, anyway.

In a way, my scarf represents a watershed. Certainly, it was after this prize bundle that I started thinking that winning stuff was highly agreeable, and that maybe I should look into making it happen more often.

That said, it's probably best not to imbue it with too much significance given that it took me another four years to really pull my finger out.

The final nudge came from a piece in the Money Saving Expert newsletter when I was juggling childcare and part-time employment. Looking for a way to make Christmas easier, I figured that if I entered enough giveaways, I'd soon be drowning in iPads, tellies and protein shakes (spoiler: didn't happen).

In other words, I made the choice to be lucky.

Initially, I figured luck was no more than a numbers game, and to be sure, if you enter hundreds of comps every day, wins will eventually ensue. Your conversion rate might not be awesome, but if you're sipping bottomless mai-tais while the sun sets on Tahiti beach, so what?

Well, I went down that path, completing every entry form I could find, and sure enough, six weeks later all I had to show was RSI and a pack of temporary tattoos. Worse still, the experience flushed my enthusiasm right down the toilet and out with the fatbergs.

It turns out I don't mix well with forms – any sort of form really, although application forms are the worst. At best, they bore me; at worst they depress me. In either case, they chip away my soul till my brain collapses in on itself due to cerebral subsidence. Possibly it's because I don't see things so black and white; possibly my thinking is too lateral for silos; possibly I'm just an overthinker. Case in point.

Even with Roboform, Fillr or any other magic form-filling app, typing and retyping my address a hundred-odd times in a single sitting really puts my mojo through the mangle. It takes a special kind of focus that I simply lack.

There's also the uncomfortable truth that if you've found a giveaway on any of the competition sites out there, then so have thousands of other people, meaning that the odds of winning it are microscopic.

So how was it that some people were winning *and* having fun but I was doing neither? Where was Yoda when I needed him?

Well, the first thing you need to know about Yoda is that he's a fictional character. If you really thought a muppet with a glowstick could teach you how to ace prize draws, then I can only apologise for not letting you down more gently. There's also the fact that if Yoda were actually flesh and blood, at tie-breakers really suck ass he would.

Back in the real world then, the go-to sherpa of comping is Di Coke (or Superlucky Di, if you prefer your sobriquets with a side order of syllables). At the time of going to press, Di hasn't won a kitchen sink, but that aside, she's won almost everything else, including a car, various holidays and a device for sucking the snot out of snouts. In other words, she's the sharpest cookie in the jar.

Within the comping community, hallowed is Di's name – not just because of her success, but also for the generosity with which Di shares her expertise. Her book, *Superlucky Secrets*, is essential reading for anyone looking to start comping, while her blog, superlucky.me, is one of the most comprehensive resources a comper could hope for. Pretty much everything I – and thousands of other compers – know about comping is thanks to Di. Without Di, I wouldn't have made it through my first year of comping. Without Di, I certainly wouldn't be writing this book.

With this in mind, I'm going to level with you: if you want advice, go see Di. This book you're holding right now won't make you smarter – it's a barely coherent stream of consciousness from a perfectly ordinary comper.

Sorry, I thought I mentioned that. I'm no power comper. For the absence of doubt, I've had a few nice wins, but if it's back-to-back winning stories you're after, then check out the amazing Rebecca Beesley's *Overcoming the Odds*. In fact, loads of people are better at this than I am – I just happen to make more noise.

So, what makes a power comper? Well, there's a direct correlation between dedication and success: in this game, you make your own luck. Sure, I could win more, but I'd have to try harder, and I'm not sure I'm up for that – after all, to everyone their own equilibrium, right?

Yes and no.

Yes, because if you're not having fun, it's absolutely time to stop. No, because sometimes it's just a case of fine-tuning your technique.

I was pondering this just recently so conducted a quick poll on Facebook to see how many comps folks enter every week, and how well they do.

Lest I offend any statisticians out there, when I say 'quick poll', I mean a small convenience sample that totally fails to represent the wider comping community, and likewise fails to use mathematically consistent units (after all, it's possible to complete a whole bunch of entry forms in the time it takes to finish one tie-break or tap out a droll anecdote); in short, the kind of survey that obtains data good enough for spurious hypotheses and quack statistickery, but little more. However, since such data is quite sufficient for the Great British press, it'll be perfectly adequate for our present needs.

Indeed, for the purposes of this piece, all we need to know is that the best result was a reported win rate of 1.6 per cent; the worst, 0.03 per cent. Well, a couple of outliers did report a win rate of nil, but I'm assuming this was for dramatic effect. In any case, the mean win rate was under 1 per cent.

So what does that mean?

On the one hand, I can take solace that my win rate isn't so bad. It doesn't top 1 per cent, but it could be much worse. On the other hand, if I want to average an extra prize a week, elementary maths suggests I'll have to comp at least 100 per cent harder.

Or will I? The other interesting thing I observed was that those compers who entered the most competitions tended to have the lowest win rate.

While this observation absolutely doesn't reflect win value, it is an advert for focusing your game. Indeed, the person with the best win rate reported entering about 30 comps a day, but winning 15–20 prizes a month. How did she do it? By focusing on two things: creative comps and wishlist comps.

Now, as the person who conducts your annual review will tell you, no one has weaknesses – just scope for improvement. So, if someone more successful than I kindly shares the source of their magnificence, I figure they're pretty much spoon-feeding me opportunities for development.

Identifying the areas for improvement is one thing. Making objectives specific, meaningful, attainable, realistic and trackable is quite another (I promise this is the last time I will *ever* talk about SMART targets of my own volition).

Take creative comps, for example. I was pretty sure there wasn't much more I could do: I'm a member of a

Facebook group for creative/effort comps and regularly check the Loquax and PrizeFinder sites too. I may not have the wit or skill to enter everything I find, but I certainly enter what I can. I must have scratched my scalp for a good half hour until into my head popped those three little words that everyone longs to hear: 'comment to win'. Two minutes later, that search string was part of my daily bookmarked searches.

As for wishlist comps – this area has never been my strong point. For starters, my wishlist tends to lack definition – I might as well type 'win nice stuff' into Google. Secondly, I just don't try hard enough. True, any basic giveaway listed on the main prize sites is going to have thousands of entries, but the bottom line is simple (if clichéd): you have to be in it to win it. So, I took the basic and bleedin' obvious step of defining my targets and then actually working towards them.

To this end, I now have bookmarked searches for everything from spa breaks and Macbooks to wellies and razors. True, I'm still waiting for most of these to translate to prizes, but in terms of finding low-entry comps, this investment in time has paid dividends, with my best result so far being a competition for an electric toothbrush that – besides me – had just the one entrant. And yes, I did win.

In closing then, it bears repeating that throwing more hours at this game isn't necessarily the answer. Sure, if you want a hardcore comping session, then go for it. Enter hundreds a night if that works for you – to a certain extent it's a numbers game after all. But if all you want is a bit of fun, it makes sense to look for a way to tighten those odds. There might not be as many tellies and games consoles, but everyone needs protein bars and gin, don't they?

Comping is fantastically scalable – if you've only time for a five-minute micro-session, that's long enough for some mindless Instagram comps, where the random draws are less opaque than those for Twitter comps, putting Joe Average with a hundred followers on the same footing as a blogger with five thousand.

The bottom line is that everyone has something they can improve. That said, it's best not to try and change everything at once: no power-lifter bench-pressed 400 pounds on their first trip to the gym – improvements come in increments.

Christmas

For compers, December is the best of times, the worst of times. At no other time of the year are so many prizes available. At no other time of the year is the competition so intense. December is to comping what a yard of eggnog is to session drinking: novel for a while, but unwise to finish – and by God will you hurt if you try.

That more companies run giveaways in December is no surprise – all marketers love a seasonal clambake, and in terms of consumer retail, nothing beats Christmas. However, what turns the season into an absolute orgy of comping is the *literally* hundreds of promoters with an advent calendar of comps – daily giveaways that last just 24 hours. Some run for twelve days of Christmas, others the whole 24. Hundreds today, hundreds tomorrow. Hundreds a day for weeks.

Day after day, day after day, hundreds of samey web-forms and social media comps all ask the same questions – what's your favourite Christmas song, the best thing about Christmas, the worst thing you've ever unwrapped? Show us your Christmas jumper, your tree, your baubles. What's your biggest Christmas fail? Retell the nativity story with emojis. Make a Christmas pudding out of haikus. You get the picture.

It's a marathon event. Some compers love it; others won't touch it with ski-pole. Newbies, however, have no idea what's about to hit them. It doesn't matter how many times you've read Di Coke's tips for the advent season (and believe me, you'll want to), you'll still not be prepared.

December 2014 was my first advent season. Despite having only a few months under my belt, thanks to Di's tips I was relatively coordinated and pretty efficient. I felt confident and I comped *hard*.

'Hard' is of course relative: I comped much harder than I'd ever done before – not as hard as some folks, certainly – but well beyond my natural appetite.

I was putting so much effort into chasing that winning buzz that if I wasn't comping, I was itching to get back to it, to tick off the ever-growing list of draws closing that day. Those comps were on my mind *a lot*. And when the season came to an end, I was bereft. It was Christmas Day, and instead of getting stuck into the festive cheer, I sat there all fidgetty, thinking, 'Damn! What do I do now?!' That hole lasted well into January, accompanied by an extended period of winter blues, the likes of which I'd never known. Gradually, I went numb. I didn't want to do anything – much less another competition.

There were, of course, other factors contributing to my funk (not least the sleep deprivation associated with having small children), but anyone who has seen gambling addiction first-hand will recognise the signs of compulsive behaviour.

If there's a hierarchy of addiction, then comping isn't really on a par with gambling; the fact that one stakes time rather than money makes it less obviously destructive. Nevertheless, as with any compulsive behaviour, the pernicious potential stands. Winning feels great, so it's understandable that people like winning as often as possible. But if you're robotically punding through entry forms or starting to neglect your housework or your family just to squeeze in a few more entries, then what was once a hobby has become an obsession, and it's time for a break. To borrow the words from the Gamble Aware campaign – when the fun stops, stop. You can't enter every competition, so don't even try!

Since that first advent, I've kept a far closer eye on both my appetite and my technique, and since that first advent, I've not only had more luck – I've also had no symptoms of addiction.

Still, it's probably best not to rest on my laurels. The real test will come in 2022 when a perfect storm of comping madness will be unleashed thanks to FIFA scheduling the World Cup to start late November and continue through most of the advent season.

The bedlam will start with the inevitable prediction competitions, which will thankfully become less time-consuming as matters progress. Next up will be the major promotions run by the official sponsors and partners, followed by the smaller, and more carefully worded giveaways run by ambush marketers. Finally, depending on how England progress, there will be scatterings of flash comps.

Within the world of comping, prediction comps make for a rum old beast. Regular compers tend to avoid them, possibly because they're too much effort, while the armchair pundits who know their onion-bags tend to find the bookies more appealing. As a result, they get surprisingly few entrants, many of whom lose interest once the knockout stage begins.

In 2014, the Brazil Tourism Board opened up its prediction comp to pretty much anyone, anywhere. Over a hundred prizes were being given away, from vouchers to cameras to various Apple products. I didn't make the top twenty, but still copped an iPod Nano, which was awesome – well, apart from the £30 of import duty I had to pay to receive it.

I found another prediction comp for the 2018 tournament. What I hadn't clocked, however, was that the score prediction aspect was purely for fun, and that the question you had to bat away before entering said predictions was actually the tie-breaker for that round.

You can therefore imagine my surprise when the promoter mailed to let me know that my throwaway comment – '5.30' – was one of the most creative responses to the question, 'At what point of the working day are you most on top of your game?'

Any criticism you may wish to throw at the weakness of that response is well deserved – I dread to imagine the quality of the rest of the field that week. Still, if ever there was an example of 'got to be in it to win it', this was it. And, in the spirit of looking for takeaways, it was also a reminder of the importance of reading instructions.

In any case, I upped my game for the last few rounds. And yes, the renewed efforts did pay off, as I made it into the top three for the final two rounds, giving me almost a ton to spend on sportswear.

Invariably, the official sponsors have the most exciting prizes during the football season; however, there are so many comps from companies that want to join in the excitement, but lack the deep pockets of megacompanies like Visa or McDonald's. In the most recent tournament, I won a football shirt on Instagram from a simple tag-and-follow comp that had barely a dozen entries. In 2014, meanwhile, I walked away with an official England shirt thanks to Carpetright, and from another promoter, a tee-shirt of Archie Gemmill scoring against Holland in 1978 – which rounds out my heritage neatly.

That England shirt has served me well – not because I enjoy sartorial statements of nationalism, but rather because it's super light-weight and doesn't cling when my sweaty bulk stumbles round the badminton court. It's also handy for entering football-related competitions, and to this end finally hit the back of the net when I won a giftcard and football from Screwfix for posting my best football cheer to Instagram.

Considering that Screwfix was an official sponsor of the ITV coverage of the tournament, surprisingly few people were entering its comps. Its daily Facebook giveaways were (as I discovered too late) getting fewer than 200 entrants, while its Instagram comp had barely a dozen. So, you can be sure I will be checking out all the TV partners in 2022.

In the UK at least, no other sporting event attracts the same volume of comps from ambush marketers – not the Rugby World Cup, not the Olympics and not even the Cooper's Hill Cheese-Rolling and Wake. For this reason, I'll be getting my Tweetdeck house in order ready for all those flash comps that will appear should England enjoy another charmed passage through the tournament.

What I'm really hoping for, however, is that by 2022, my first-born will be able to sit through an entire match without bringing someone to tears.

Dry season

Abstemiousness never goes out of fashion. Well, not in January anyway. Some folks give up the sauce for the month, others try their hand at veganism. Come January 2015, I was in comping detox. It wasn't an active decision, but once the low mood set in, I couldn't face picking up the tools and starting over. It doesn't take long to learn that if you don't enter anything, you don't win anything.

Thus began my first dry spell. As rites of passage go, it could have been better timed, but it was mercifully short compared with some of those I've endured since.

The fact is, for all dry patches are no fun, they're part of the game, and as with any setback in life, learning to cope is an essential part of growing. True, this one was self-inflicted. Mostly, however, they are a matter of statistical inevitability: no one wins more than they lose.

Comping isn't for pessimists – it's a hair-shirt woven of disappointments. I've been two streets away from winning the Free Postcode Lottery and two car-lengths away from the My Lucky Patch jackpot, but that doesn't make me unlucky – it's simply a lack of *good* luck. Had one of these lucky neighbours clipped off my wing-mirror without telling me, then yep, that might have been unlucky. But the absence of something – in this case good luck – does not make it a negative.

Some people grumble about the dry season, as if that will swing things back in their favour. Well, stop me if I'm stating the obvious, but there are more productive ways to spend that time and energy.

Successful compers don't rely on the odds alone; they also have a positive mental attitude. In other words, when they find themselves in the midst of a dry spell, they use it as an opportunity to improve rather than waste time dwelling on the perceived failure.

For instance, when I'm relieved of the delicious burden of updating my spreadsheet of wins and sending thank-you messages to promoters, it means I have more time for other comping-related activities, such as chatting with my comping buddies, finding new compers to ~~stalk~~ follow on social media, and investing in the various comping groups I've joined, whether that involves sharing comps, notifying winners or discussing best practice – whatever's appropriate. It's all good karma.

More practically, I revisit my skeleton routine – the things I can do on autopilot when my brain's not in the right place but I want to maintain some semblance of comping normality. For me, that's basically opening a set of comping bookmarks (local comp searches and daily lotteries, maybe even some wishlist searches). These bookmarks take seconds to open and, at most, minutes to close. Anything I do on top of this – whether catching up with Facebook groups or hashtag searching on Instagram – is a bonus.

And if I've really got time on my hands, well, that's the perfect opportunity to learn a new skill to improve the technical side of my comping. Snapchat, for example, seems to overhaul its interface on a weekly basis, so there's invariably at least one social media platform I need to learn from scratch. Likewise, there's any number of tutorials out there that I can use to improve my grasp of Twitter and its extended family of plugins, such as Tweetdeck or Hootsuite.

Then there's the admin. My Twitter feed is a barrage of jibber jabber, so I'll review my follows and remove any that are no longer of interest. My Facebook feed is similarly cacophonous, but here things get more tricky –

while Facebook is happy to unlike pages off its own bat, it appears less keen for users to do so under their own steam. Sure, you can unfollow pages as and when they come into your newsfeed, or go to your likes page and unlike to your heart's content, but either way, the process is plodding and painful. It's a sorry reminder that if you're not paying for something, then you're not the customer – you're the product being sold. It's also a reminder of why I tend to avoid Facebook comps in the first place.

Finally, Instagram. Until the middle of 2016, follows were listed in chronological order, making it relatively easy to thin out old, redundant profiles. All that changed when Instagram introduced the wantonly opaque system we see today, where the profiles appear to be tossed in with scant regard for any kind of order. I've heard that the desktop version of the site still shows follows in a vaguely chronological order, but given that the human race evolves faster than one can scroll through this list, and the fact that the process of unfollowing is so frequently unreliable, I prefer not to go there. For this reason, my daily feed now consists of approximately 1,600 pictures I have no wish to see.

Tempting as a humungous unliking bender sounds, however, I'm reluctant to head down that path as such behaviour is often associated with automated tools that can contravene the various social media platforms' terms of use, and the suspension of my account is something I'm anxious to avoid.

The admin doesn't stop there, of course. I've got folders of stock photography in desperate need of review – from Christmas jumper pics to goofy selfies to goodness knows what. As some photographic competitions appear with seasonal inevitability, I sometimes take new pictures in anticipation; and if I'm feeling really time-rich, I might even look through my old video footage to see if anything can be repurposed.

At the same time, I take solace in the fact being lucky isn't confined to my track record with giveaways, and I celebrate any and all luck as I find it. Sometimes that takes the form of really random luck, like the time a promoter was so tickled by one of my lad's bizarre birthday lists I'd posted on Instagram that they got in touch in order to send him a really lovely gift themselves, but equally, if the till rings up lower than I was expecting or I discover a new cheese, then such fortune is also worth minor jubilation.

Last time I was laid up on doctor's orders, I had two whole days to think about how to improve my comping game. That's not to say I recommend minor surgery as a route to improving one's winning streak, but if I'm gifted an opportunity, I'm not one to look it in the mouth.

Finally, while there's naught to gain from mourning what might have been; there is everything to gain from reflecting and persevering. For example, if I've not won a particular creative competition, I'll ask myself: What went well? What could have gone better? What can I learn from the winner?

In short, I draw on the advice of that lamentably tired sign and keep calm and carry on.

Effort

It is a fact universally acknowledged that a single prize draw in possession of complex entry mechanic will inevitably attract fewer entrants.

It's not simply that people are lazy – although it is undoubtedly easier to follow and retweet than to learn some arbitrary and ultimately pointless skill and then demonstrate it in front of the camera, like some kind of budget Generation Game contestant. There's also the prevailing misconception that a lack of skills is some kind of obstacle to success. For example, when it comes to dancing, I cut a rug with all the grace of a giraffe on ice, but that hasn't stopped me winning a bucket-load of cheddar and a couple of tickets to watch Beyoncé slay. I've likewise been rewarded for writing highly disposable poetry about stationery and business away-days when everyone else either had stage-fright or simply couldn't be bothered.

When I wrote one limerick, for example, I was up against fewer than ten entrants – and half of them either went completely off-topic or forgot to make their entry scan. That effort won me a £20 giftcard to blow at Rymans.

My initial thought was to splash out on a new inkjet cartridge, but while ink might be more expensive than champagne, it is by some margin the inferior treat.

It then dawned on me that while winning essentials is fabulous, winning fabulous things is unquestionably fabulouser. And, in terms of modestly priced non-essentials, the electric pencil sharpener is surely the fabuloustest of all. You want a benchmark? I've previously won an iPad Mini, and compared with the electric pencil sharpener, it didn't change a single atom of my life.

Owning an electric pencil sharpener is a life-changing experience. It's zen in a plastic case. If you're scoffing right now, I bet you don't have small children who can't yet be trusted to sharpen their own pencils, and you've never experienced the wrist-ache that follows a full pencil-box sharpening session. I'm through the looking glass now.

I've entered tie-breakers, photo comps, dad-joke comps, blog-writing comps, Pinterest board comps – I've even won a prize for my Fuzzy Felt skills. But so far so pedestrian. What has me at hello, is any competition with a novel entry mechanic. As a matter of fact, the more fun it is to enter the comp, the less I care what the prize is – and sometimes about winning full stop.

Buxton Water ran such a promotion, with goodie bags for the first 50 people to tweet video evidence of them flipping a Buxton Water bottle along with the #buxtonflip hashtag. The video with the most retweets also won a much bigger prize, but I didn't pay that part much mind as (a) it was tickets for something I couldn't attend and (b) if my wife had wanted to spend her free time watching adolescent behaviour she'd have offered her pupils weekend revision classes.

While I tend not to buy into purchase-necessary competitions, in this instance my first-born was already pestering for a plastic bottle to lob around the back yard, so I figured this one might also buy me a half-hour of peace. As it happens, it was a mere five minutes, but peace is peace, right?

After a few practice flips, I captured some passable footage and called the lad in, flipping the bottle once more – looking, for all intents and purposes, like I'd pulled it off first time. Momentarily speechless with awe, he looked at me like I was some kind of god. What can I say – seven-year olds are easily impressed, and as a parent, you've got to get your jollies.

And indeed, further jollies ensued a week later with the delivery of a tee-shirt, USB stick, iPhone case, earphone case, keyring containing a disposable shower poncho, and a rubbery trumpet accessory that makes phones marginally louder when on speaker mode.

Out of interest, I did a quick sweep for the #buxtonflip hashtag just a few days later. As far as I can tell, less than half the prizes were given out, providing a textbook example of the extent to which odds can shorten once a little effort is required.

Then of course there are the comps that pull you in by preying on your compulsive instincts. The Great Oreo Cookie Quest was one of those comps.

This app-based promotion was basically a scavenger hunt where you had no idea what you were looking for. Actually, that's unfair – there were daily clues, but in many respects it was quicker simply to point your phone at anything and everything and hope for the best.

In hindsight, this promotion should have had a health warning for obsessive compulsives, as the pleasure (read: sense of relief) associated with collecting items grew exponentially the further you progressed. This was in no small part down to the fact that some of the items were nigh impossible to scan.

Take milk, for example. It must have taken me an hour to scan this one.

At this point in the game, I had fewer than ten items to collect, while the player in pole position had only one. So ... everything to play for, right?

It had taken a few hours to get this far, and was plainly going to take hours more. By all rights, I should have conducted some sort of cost-benefit exercise with my time, but by this point logic had plainly gone out the window. By hook or by crook, I was scanning that milk.

Thankfully, a kind-hearted fellow comper put me out of my misery with the following recommendation: froth it up a little and snap from above.

Ker-ching! Item scanned!

I must have spent just as long fumbling with Google Image Search, trying to find a hatchet that would scan – no easy task when the app thinks they're all axes. My doggedness paid off eventually, but when I realised I now had to scan an ice axe as well, my heart sank. I must have pointed my phone at a hundred ice axes, only to have the app think they were hammers, nails or, on one occasion, a stethoscope.

By now, I'd reached seventh place on the national leaderboard – woohoo! Unfortunately, the player who had been leading the pack had managed to find the last item on the list. Game over, in other words. Except for the fact that I hadn't checked the T&C at this point, and spent another couple of hours banging my head against the wall, trying to scan pliers and coconuts before having the common sense to check the small print.

By the time I downed tools, there were three items I'd failed to scan, and a further three I'd failed to identify at all. Which was more frustrating I couldn't say; however, the sense of calm as the burden was lifted was blissfully overwhelming.

For £15 of Google Play vouchers, was the effort really worth it? That's nothing – sometimes I enter competitions with absolutely no intention of winning. That's not to say I enter for prizes I actively don't want; rather, I like the brief so much that I enter for the joy of the challenge, without the slightest hope of winning or worrying what I could have done better to impress the judges.

One such example was for a competition to win flights to Malta that required entrants to post a story about Malta on their blog. I got my mum to narrate a retro slideshow of photos from my childhood holidays. I can't imagine it ticked many boxes for the promoter, but it made my mum and my sister so happy to reminisce about those holidays – and about happier times with my dad, that it was reward in itself.

I've likewise written entries for creative writing competitions that have veered so far from the brief that they've been quite unusable. I then end up saving my work in my own little creative writing folder, before butchering the text into something vaguely in line with what the promoter has asked for. The result is a blatant hack job, as by this point it's invariably too late to do anything about it. But I can live with that – I've got the director's cut on file, ready to use in a way that suits me, some time in the future.

My dad used to say that sometimes it's better to travel than to arrive. I could dedicate hours and hours of my life to the completion of entry forms, but when the grind of that mindless toil is over, what's left? God willing, some prizes, the value of which might even be vaguely proportional to the hours invested in winning them. But beyond the material goods? Again, I confess, none of my fondest memories relate to web forms or retweets.

Winning might be the most obvious benefit of this hobby, but it isn't the only one.

First time

Every journey has its milestones, some of which make better copy than others. For example, there's only so much spin you can put on being the only entrant in a Twitter comp to win a branded beanie hat from a company specialising in cattle disinfectant.

You could say my journey started in the summer term of 1989, which would have made me 14. A chap from Cambridge University Press came into our English class to talk about something – I'm guessing publishing, but the memories are hazy – for all I know, it was the mating habits of the Palawan stink badger.

At the end of this clearly memorable session, we were, as was the norm, set our weekly homework. What made this week different, however, was that (a) it would take five minutes instead of the usual hour or more, and (b) there would be prizes.

I wasn't the kind of pupil to need reward-based incentivisation; however, I did have an admirable track record when it came to rushing my homework to get my parents off my back. Thus, when I was tasked with writing a story in a sentence, it was as good as giving me a week off.

Mine wasn't the best entry. The best entry (I later learned) was plagiarised from Stephen King. The judges clearly suspected something was afoot, however, and awarded first prize – a concise Chambers Dictionary – to my hastily tossed off guff about a radioactive worm. (Stephen King, meanwhile, bagged a mere pocket dictionary.)

I still have the dictionary. The dust-jacket is long since perished, of course, and the spine flaps around in the draft, and if you want the skinny on latte or for that matter any other contemporary term such as LOL, vape or emoji, it's plainly no use at all. That said, if I want slumpflation or perestroika, then it's totally my go-to reference book.

I'll be honest though, it's not the win that got me into this game. Half my class didn't bother with the homework, so I didn't feel like I'd won fair and square. What's more, the plagiarism wasn't even confessed for another couple of years, so I simply couldn't understand how I could possibly have beaten a pseudonymised Stephen King. It didn't sit right.

Oh the innocence! I love that it never even occurred to me that someone might cheat. But more than that, it makes me laugh that I didn't value my win because the odds weren't long enough. Coming from someone who high-fived himself after scoring a cow soap beanie against zero opposition, that really is incredible.

Fast-forward then some twenty-five years later when I'd decided to give this game a proper go. My first prize I forget – it took a few more before I felt comfortable self-identifying as a 'comper'. Before I started using a spreadsheet to record my wins, my discipline was all over the shop, and the best I could say was that I dabbled. What I do remember, however, was my first big win – a ridiculously fancy cartridge for my record player and a hundred quid record token to blow on vinyl. Having never previously (or since) dropped a ton in a record shop, this win offered a window onto another world – a chance to pretend to be someone who was, if not enjoying life more than me, then certainly living it more. Thanks to comping, I had, as if by magic, turned into Mr Benn.

At this point, I have to confess that I'm yet to fit the cart – and predictably, I'm blaming my children. Once they annexed my airspace, and my record deck, like many other things, was relegated to occasional treat, there seemed little point in pimping it out.

That children and noise go hand in hand, we all know. Likewise, it's hardly a secret that said noise increases exponentially, the more children you add to the mix. Some people are blessed – it washes over them. Not me, however – I'm literally allergic. The consecutive (and indeed concurrent) episodes of shrieking from one child or the other have overexcited my senses such that I'm now clinically intolerant of even their tiniest squawk. Being unable to abide the incessant clanking and slurping of children at mealtimes is nothing unusual; however, the fact that I now have a doctor's note to excuse me from the table, does rather set me apart.

Right now, my happy place would be inside an immersion tank guarded by Benedictine librarian mice. And yet it was not ever thus. Indeed, there was a time when all my spare time and pennies were devoted to music. Once the wee beasties found their lungs, however, things changed.

At first, I didn't notice how much I was cowering from their hullaballoo. It started with simply switching off the radio so I didn't have to suffer the blather, and before long, not playing anything during the day as I knew I'd only be hauled out of the room to wipe another backside or resolve another fight. Eventually, it got to the point that I'd simply forget to turn on my music at all. Night after night, I'd sit in unnecessary silence – not even noticing the peace, never mind enjoying it. Come birthdays and Christmas, people would give me new CDs that I'd rinse for a couple of weeks, but somehow, it was never enough to relight my fire. The silence would always prevail.

For this reason, I'm saving the cart as a treat for when my ears have had chance to recover. When the children become less keen on bleeding me of my famous joie de vivre, I will fit it, and when I do, I will love it. And these records, which I know sound golden, will sound so hot they'll ooze into my ears like golden lava, but ideally less burny.

But where did this prize come from? Or more specifically, what was the challenge? It was a simple photo competition: show off your vinyl collection and add a little tie-break text. It didn't take long for this to turn into a pissing contest between insanely serious collectors with shelves and shelves and shelves of records. There was no way I could compete on quantity, so in keeping with the people of Norfolk doing things differently, I staged a picture with my then four-year-old son pretending to deejay with my ear defenders and a box of 45s, and added a couple of sentences about how my father's and grandfather's records were all mixed in with mine, and how my lad would be the next guardian of the family trove. It was here that I learned that while a picture may say a thousand words, the right caption can really swing it – a lesson that served me well on a couple of Pinterest comps too.

It was also here that I learned that being given licence to act like a swanky pants is surprisingly nice. That it's nice isn't the surprise; rather, it's even nicer than you expect it will be. It's a huge cake without the calories; a free bar without the hangover; an electric whisk you can lick without being judged.

So, it's no wonder that I can remember my first VIP experience in almost forensic detail.

I'd won football tickets before. Thanks to Barclays and Aviva, respectively, I'd seen Norwich hold Man City to a goalless draw (better than it sounds) and beat Rotherham 3-1. The match with Fulham, however, was the one I was *really* looking forward to. Not because it was going to be a high-stakes promotion dogfight (that much had long been written off), and not because it would be a chance to see a world-class team show off its silky skills (with all due respect, Fulham, you're no Barcelona); no – this matchday was going to be awesome because I had golden tickets. The fact that the match was a half-dead rubber was irrelevant: these tickets *guaranteed* a good time.

I won the tickets when Green Farm Coffee – sponsor of the South Stand at Carrow Road – ran a Gleam competition on its website. I already knew who I wanted to be my plus-one, so I got my mate to enter too. Thanks to this referral, I got an extra entry into the draw. Whether that was the straw that tipped the camel's back in my favour I shall never know, but for the sake of the narrative, let's just imagine it was. In any case, there weren't twenty entrants, so the odds were good.

The prize, simply put, was an afternoon of top-notch hospitality at the finest football club in East Anglia (yeah, you heard me Ipswich), comprising a tour of the ground, a generous lunch and exceedingly comfortable seats to watch the game.

Without doubt, the tour was incredible. Happy to chat both football and the business of football, our guide showed us all the special little nooks of Carrow Road, from the dugouts to the dressing rooms, the press conference suite to the post-match interview cubicles, and, lest we forget, the trophy cabinet.

While it's fair to say that Carrow Road will never rival any of the big boy clubs for silverware – let's face it, Manchester City has picked up more meaningful gongs this last year than Norwich has won in its entire existence – there were nonetheless so many stories in that one room that it was nigh impossible to digest even the highlights. But with lunch beckoning and a queue building up behind us, we had to make way for the next party to see the spoils.

Speaking of lunch, the meal was (as you'd expect from Delia's staff) impeccable: a champagne aperitif, followed by a salmon fishcake starter, succulent roast lamb main and something I'm tempted to call a bakewell cake for dessert, and – of course – coffee.

Now, about those seats. I had no idea that anyone outside of the squad was allowed a comfy seat. I acknowledge my error. At the top of the terrace, opposite the dugouts, is where the posh people sit. The view was fantastic and my riff-raff buns were over the proverbial moon.

As we got to our seats, the Barclay was in fine voice, the team having pounded Reading 7-1 in the previous game. No one was expecting a repeat of that, of course. Much like no one was expecting Fulham to go a goal up in the first five minutes. Suffice to say, I'm disinclined to discuss the subsequent 85 minutes; that is, unless you want further intel on my euphoric buttocks.

The trouble with vipping, of course, is that it's easy to get a taste for it. My only other taste of the high life has been at Wimbledon – of which more in due course – suffice to say I'm so desperate for a refresher that if the prize came with bottomless champagne and an access-all-areas lanyard, I'd cheerfully take tickets to a paint-drying exhibition.

Grails

Ghost town competitions. There's probably an official name for them in the comping community, but that's what I like to call super-low entry comps – the ones where the number of entrants doesn't even hit double figures. The comps that have flown under the radar.

From the promoter's perspective, these comps can only be frustrating – despite their best endeavours to create buzz around their brand, for whatever reason, it just hasn't happened. For the comper, however, they're like golden pots of four-leafed leprechauns at the end of the rainbow.

The Holy Grail of ghost town promotions is of course one where you're the only entrant. I've not found one for a while, but they're definitely out there. In fact, I once entered a competition that Asahi was running across both Facebook and Instagram, with a prize for each channel, and effectively won it twice. Awkward.

It was likewise embarrassing when I had to go to a local menswear store to claim my £75 voucher when I was the sole entrant in its selfie comp. To make the experience all the more excruciating, I had to return twice more before I could find anything I was remotely prepared to wear.

Understandably, promoters caught out like this won't be in a hurry to announce their winners. They're not exactly leaving the masses hanging, after all. They also have plenty of other, more pressing, demands on their time.

With notable exceptions, most people are only human, and it's all too easy for those demands to muscle their way to the top of their to-do list. Before you know it, that little job of picking a winner gets put off, postponed and sometimes even forgotten entirely.

This spell of sustained hush can be even more excruciating than waiting for a big-prize announcement – at least with big prizes, the chance of winning tends to be minimal and you may as well forget you've entered in the first place. When my odds of winning are better than one in ten, however, this kind of thing just eats me.

Worst of all, imagine a low-entry effort-based comp where the other entries are a matter of public record and you know – *you just know* – that your entry is, objectively speaking, totally well more awesome than all the rest. Patience and humility will never be so scarce.

For me, the closest to this came in May 2016, when Pilgrims Choice ran a competition to win a heap of cheese – which is to say, a heap of cheese vouchers (a year's worth of cheddar delivered on a single pallet would be a bittersweet prize, to say the least). They asked to see Joe Public's cheesy dance moves. Sadly for them, Joe Public was shy. Despite the company having many thousands of Facebook followers, only three were inclined to share a video.

The competition closed, but no winner was announced. Folks kindly asked on my behalf whether the winner had been chosen – still there was silence. I followed up on Twitter – still nothing. One of the other entrants asked too. Nada.

And so the pursuit of cheddar fell down my to-do list, displaced by the vulgar number of tedious chores associated with parenting, and by October, I'd largely forgotten the competition. Until, that is, on some hashtag day or other, I found an excuse to tweet the promoter about an altogether unrelated matter, and by way of a blag, sent them a link to my video. They liked it enough to send a few vouchers my way, blessing me with cheese and the warm sense of reassurance that, although it might not have been quite what I had in mind, at least my self-imposed humiliation hadn't all been in vain and, perhaps more importantly, I could draw a line under the whole sorry affair.

But fate snatched that pencil from my paw – a week later, the promoter contacted me through Facebook to let me know I'd won the May competition after all.

I'd love to say it was my nudge that edged it, but the very next day, one of the other entrants tweeted me her congratulations – it turned out that she too had been seeking closure, and just a couple of days prior had contacted the promoter to see if any winners had been announced.

Cheese aside, this tale provides some key takeaways – the value of perseverance being the most obvious. More importantly, however, it demonstrates that the true grail of comping is community.

To the outside ear that might sound odd – after all, isn't comping by definition a zero-sum game? Well, I suppose you could look at it like that. Or, you could look at it as a gateway to meeting people with a shared interest – an opportunity to make new friends.

You don't have to have known prolonged isolation to appreciate that having friends makes you less lonely, and being less lonely is sure-fire way of being more happy. More than that, friends inspire each other to grow – to bloom. Friendship helps people to know themselves better. In other words, friendship is a basic ingredient in positive mental health.

Since I became part of the comping community, more people have checked in on me; more people have made me laugh; and more people have sent me in the direction of free cheese. In short, I'm part of a crew, and my crew has my back. Pretty lucky, right?

Hashtags

The wise comper prepares their hashtag calendar in advance. I, however, am not wise. Recklessly negligent? Maybe; but wise? No. At a time when hashtag days outnumber regular days by a factor of three (a figure that post-truth experts anticipate will rise to five by 2021), this really is unforgiveable.

Let's be frank: no one has the first idea how many hashtag events are loitering round the internet these days. What is manifestly obvious, however, is that the volume of such days has grown to pandemic proportions, leaving many fighting for airspace (#HedgehogDay is on #GroundhogDay – who knew?). They've also become stackable, like getting a double word score in Scrabble (13 April), as seen with #WorldStationeryDay (27 April) erupting through the middle of #NationalStationeryWeek.

While some of these hashtags do have their merits – #WorldMentalHealthDay being a case in point – most hashtaggery is just marketing flannel. When it comes to comping, however, that's no bad thing. If there's one thing marketing pish means, it's flash giveaways. Of course, some may be more eagerly anticipated than others: #InternationalCoffeeDay (1 October) sounds promising; #InternationalHashtagDay (23 August) less so.

#NationalLimerickDay and #WorldPoetryDay tend to yield a fair amount of low-hanging fruit on Twitter, while #StarWarsDay gets bigger every year, as the Johnny Come Latelys clamour for a piece of the pie. Indeed, May the Fourth is now sufficiently embedded in the hive mind that Star Wars action has started to spread across Facebook too – and occasionally to interesting ends.

Searching Facebook (or for that matter, Instagram) for flash comps is of course harder than searching Twitter. For this reason, I seldom find many. Given also how many of the Facebook comps are tedious like-shares, I tend also to pay them short shrift. Show me something novel, however, and I'm all ears – such as the time when Music Magpie designed a Star Wars treasure hunt that kept me trawling its website way past my bedtime. I had a one in two chance of winning something on that occasion – and had the promoter not shifted the closing date, those odds would have been even better – but some things just aren't meant to be.

Instead, my luck was waiting for me at Hollywood Bowl, where for the second year in a row I won a Star Wars plushie for showcasing one of the many ways that comping has helped me grow as a person – in this instance, impersonating Yoda. It might not have been the most accurate of impressions, but it was more convincing than my wookie roar from the previous year.

In terms of hashtag love, #StarWarsDay is clearly top of the class. It's the comping equivalent of that sporty lad at primary school who scored all the goals, kissed all the girls and turned the class general election into a politically vacant popularity contest where a viable manifesto counts for nothing. (I'm not bitter, Paul, but we both know your promise to build the school a railway was shameless, unworkable bluster.)

At the other end of the spectrum are hashtags that resonate with the public yet somehow attract less marketing attention. A case in point is #EdBallsDay, which celebrates when the erstwhile Shadow Chancellor of the Exchequer tweeted his own name on 28 April 2011.*

Even though the #EdBallsDay hashtag has demonstrated its viral potential, surprisingly few promoters have bandwagonned it. And when I say 'few', I mean – in my personal experience – 'one' – a fact that has made my life 42 grams of protein the richer.

---

*The last time I checked, the 'Ed Balls' tech fumble had 103,957 retweets, while the corresponding cock-up by Eamonn Holmes (the 'Portugal Girlie' affair) was flatlining at 1,643. According to my calculations, this means that Balls' ballsup is approximately 63 times more amusing than a professional sofa cushion conflating Twitter with Pornhub.

If only

Back in 1946, the *Evening Standard* was paying George Orwell to write pretty much whatever popped into his head. One week, he'd be chatting about junk shops or the marvels of British cuisine, the next he'd be spouting off about how to make a cup of tea. For another of his famous essays, he invented a fictitious pub, known as The Moon Under Water, and went on to describe, in forensic detail, what made this boozer so great. While much of his argument was informed by nothing more than the idiosyncrasies of his own drinking habits, it's worth noting that his chief affection was for the atmosphere of the establishment, thus making it abundantly clear that he wasn't referring to the Wetherspoons pubs of the same name.

Although Orwell was a man of copious opinions, he wasn't to my knowledge a comper. This is a shame, as it leaves a great literary hole in the canon of comping. While I'm not the man to fill that hole, I can at least pay homage to Orwell in the best way I can – by telling you about the fabulous competitions run by The Moon Under Water.

The promoters at The Moon Under Water have seen comps on Instagram that fail to mention that they are being run on multiple channels, and they feel this is at best ambiguous and at worst misleading. For this reason, The Moon Under Water promotes its giveaways across all its media channels. It has pinned posts on Twitter and Facebook, as well as attractive creative on Instagram. All these posts direct potential entrants to its website, where every last detail about each competition can be found in its full glory – the entry mechanic, the prize, the T&C – the lot.

The Moon Under Water wants people to engage with its brand. It wants to embed its name in people's minds so that everyone who has taken part – even if they haven't won – will associate The Moon Under Water with happy memories. For this reason, it never asks entrants to mindlessly like and share or follow and retweet, because it knows entrants will have already forgotten its name in the time it takes to fulfil those actions. Likewise, it never directs entrants through a mystery tour of allied companies it would like them to follow as it knows this will dampen enthusiasm for its brand. It also never obliges entrants to click through a dozen Gleam or Rafflecopter entry widgets, as it knows that ticking boxes is no way to engender brand love.

For this reason, The Moon Under Water always runs effort-based competitions. Sometimes it invites entrants to create an original – and impossible to plagiarise – photograph with a certain item, or something that corresponds with its latest marketing campaign, be that seasonal (say, Christmas) or activity-based (say, jumping for joy). Certainly, whenever it asks for a selfie, it publishes T&C that define *exactly* what the word 'selfie' constitutes.

From time to time, its competitions require entrants to submit a brief video clip: sometimes something simple and silly such as mixing the promoter's name into a tongue twister; sometimes more demanding, such as a sketch or a monologue, that – again – resonates with its latest marketing campaign.

The Moon Under Water also loves tie-breaks – indeed, its company slogan was originally coined via a tie-break competition.

Entries are always limited to one per person. No one gets additional credit for tagging more people, reposting the competition or kissing promoter ass.

Winners are never decided by public vote. Rather, winning entries are judged by an independent third party. Furthermore, winners are contacted directly rather than announced, untagged in a social media post.

The Moon Under Water never extends the deadlines for its competitions. They always close on a defined date – rather than, say, at 10,000 followers. Likewise, winners are always announced as scheduled. Winning entries are published on all social media feeds, and, where possible, old posts promoting the competition updated to point to the announcement.

Sometimes prizes are big; sometimes they are small. But whatever their size, they are relevant to the brand and both delightful and useful to the winner. When The Moon Under Water produces merchandise, its mugs are artful, its pens built to last. More often though, it gives away its own product or gift vouchers (as opposed to discount codes) for its online shop, as it knows this will encourage genuine word-of-mouth enthusiasm about its brand. And from time to time, it also partners with like-minded brands to provide bigger – but, crucially – congruous prizes. These additional prizes always complement The Moon Under Water's product and its present marketing campaign, whether that be in the form of traditional concepts, such as champagne and chocolate for Valentine's Day, or immersive horror experiences to tie up with Halloween.

What it doesn't do is give away iPads for the sake of it. Competitions to win iPads are great, but they are ten a penny. They also have no congruence with the Moon Under Water brand. Instead, each prize is carefully considered for the unique circumstances of the promotional campaign in question.

Perhaps you know of a promoter such as The Moon Under Water, or one that runs giveaways with even greater panache. If so, I should be glad to hear of it!

Job

'Get paid £20 an hour as a professional competition enterer.'

It wasn't April Fool's Day when I read this, but it might as well have been – the idea of being a professional comper (or even competition enterer) is a nonsense.

The article continued:

'Pros must find at least five competitions an hour and, if possible, enter them.'

Where to begin? The idea of taking just over ten minutes to complete an entry form sets the bar so low as to make it a trip hazard. With a work rate like that, you wouldn't get return on investment even if you paid minimum wage. Given also that third-party entries are generally forbidden, this hypothetical employer would also be disqualified for breaching terms and conditions.

'The service launches thanks to increased demand for professional "compers", as it's revealed many can quit their jobs thanks to competition success.'

Who exactly are these *many* people – and who is revealing them? Yes, there are people without conventional salaried employment who devote a lot of time to comping, and who may even be really successful, but you can't pay the mortgage with nut butter and Nutribullets. Lottery winners might quit their jobs. Compers, not so much.

Things like this fox me something silly. On the face of it, the article promoting this 'job' seemed perfectly serious. At the same time, someone was plainly having a laugh.

On closer inspection, however, it turned out that the agency advertising the position was the same one that had previously claimed it was possible to earn upwards of £45ph plus expenses as a professional McDonald's Monopoly player. Naturally I'd have been first in line for the gig had I not been so busy piloting their pigs.

But truth never has enjoyed the same popularity as a good story, has it? Certainly not among the Great British press, anyway. In this regard, the story about the Russian teen who won a month-long hotel stay with a pornstar springs to mind. According to the Telegraph, it was his prize for being the 100,000th person to visit Cases4Real, a website selling virtual weapons for video games. Needless to say, the lad was 'delighted' and his mum was 'furious' (sample quote: 'He is studying ... They should give us 100,000 roubles [£931] instead').

As for the boy's father, he was quoted elsewhere as saying he will 'take possession of the prize himself, as the boy's legal guardian'.

Wow.

Well, nearly wow.

The fact that no terms and conditions were ever published for this so-called competition was always a bit fishy; and the fact that the boy was an actor made it fishier still. But facts are like fondue sets aren't they? Whimsical relics venerated by cranks and retrophiles. If the story sounds too good, too amazing or too ridiculous to be true, well, that doesn't mean it isn't, right?

For example, when someone out of the blue offers you £3000 to lick the feet of complete strangers, what sort of a muggins wastes good licking time getting their facts straight? Such was the case in 2017 when a prankster convinced the manager of a Poundworld store to recruit two customers and humiliate them as part of a team training exercise that also involved drawing on their faces and riding them like ponies.

Clearly, the mere mention of a prize can lead to some very unfortunate decision making. In March 2018, for example, one Staffordshire woman became so fixated on winning a family holiday to Florida that she convinced her husband to get an iffy tattoo of Ant and Dec. Within hours, their show (and with it the competition) had been cancelled following Ant's arrest for drink driving.

To be fair, many people have done ridiculous things on the off chance of winning a trip to Florida. A quick search for the hashtag #FacesforFlorida on Twitter or Instagram will return copious images of wishful compers sacrificing decorum in the hope of getting to the Sunshine State. Of these images, me, sitting on a Vauxhall Astra, dressed as a tweedy Don Johnson, chest hairs blowing in the January breeze, is one of the least remarkable. I might not have been among the winners, but unlike the young lady being basted with jam, at least I didn't need to be hosed down after my photo shoot.

Of course, bizarre decisions are by no means the preserve of those entering competitions. Back in 2015, Grandmaster Flash's promotions team ran a Facebook competition where you had to guess Flash's five favourite hip hop records. The answers weren't hard to find – the intel was all in his recent Twitter feed; the problem was that most of the songs weren't hip hop.

I figured that this wasn't the time to split hairs, so I fed the promoter the songs listed on Twitter and crossed my fingers. Happily it was the right call.

The story didn't end there, however. I knew the prize comprised a Puma track-top and trainers; I also knew that (for reasons not shared with me) it was going to take considerably longer than the average four weeks for the prize to arrive. Eventually, all became clear: the prize was not being handled by the Puma marketing team, but rather by Flash's wardrobe crew. The jacket and shoes arrived in the UK with the rest of his tour gear – it turned out I'd won an official (and I'm pretty sure money-can't-buy) Grandmaster Flash track-top.

To add to the madness, the promoter didn't courier the prize to me. Rather, a despatch driver was hired to bring it up from central London to Norwich – no doubt as would have happened had the kit been for Flash himself.

Having only ever worked in places where you'd be roasted for using a C4 envelope when a C5 would have been quite sufficient, this was a fascinating insight into A-list profligacy. I definitely felt less frivolous about the time I used up my first-class stamp stash to despatch my Christmas cards rather than buy a half-dozen second-class ones.

Another promoter to break with conventional thinking, albeit on a far grander scale, is Cadbury. In 2018, its Hunt the White Egg promotion – a scavenger hunt plagiarised from the world of Willy Wonka, but with additional *ick* in the golden ticket – incentivised product contamination on an unprecedented scale. Exactly how much stock had to be destroyed due to unauthorised unwrapping is anyone's guess. Of greater concern, however, is how much should have been destroyed but was consumed instead.

For reasons no hygienic person will ever fathom, the campaign returned in 2019. I begged off. But only because no one was willing to hire a Professional Creme Egg Tamperer.

Kids

Never work with children or animals. I've tried both. Which is worse, I couldn't say: my cat by her very nature cannot, does not and will not cooperate; my first-born likewise.

That's an exaggeration – there was that time when he was four. Since then, however, his behaviour has – as they say – explored boundaries. Combined with his extreme control-freakery, he's not a natural at taking direction, generally only playing ball once he sees the tears in your eyes.

The net result is that every time I try to recruit him for a video comp, it turns into a complete ordeal, with my wife asking why I keep putting myself though this. It's madness, I know, but I can't help but cling to the moments of glory he's had in front of the camera. When he turns on the charm, it's magnetic. I know I would say that – I'm his dad after all – but I'm not the only person to have said so.

For example, after Brush-Baby sent him and his brother electric toothbrushes and some rather novel toothpaste to road-test, he thanked them by video. Brush-Baby loved his performance so much they built a whole blog post around it and then sent him another couple of years' worth of toothpaste and brushes to thank him.

For any parent, these are beautiful moments – not because of the toothpaste, although that is a bonus – but because seeing your kid be the best they can be makes you feel, at last, like you're doing it right. What's more, you've committed all the evidence to file, so once you've viewed it *ad nauseam*, you can bore your friends with it too.

Thus, it's with this in mind that I keep convincing myself that if I chuck a kid or two into my video then the judges will love it. Sadly, and much to the boy's frustration, the results don't bear that out, making him even more reluctant to cooperate next time, meaning that the next video is even more likely to miss the mark. It's a vicious circle. The cat, at least, is always consistently uncooperative.

There's also the problem that having put in the effort, he feels the prize should be guaranteed. I get that. In the aforementioned case of the toothbrushes, he already had the reward in his hands. When it comes to a competition, however, it's all very well offering a child commission, but that level of delayed gratification is generally too abstract for your average eight year-old.

For any comper, failing to win an entry-form or like-retweet comp is not simply a doddle; it's also emotionally straightforward as there's little to no investment. When you've spent hours on an entry but fail to make the podium, however, it's disappointing, no matter how old you are. And more effort equals more disappointment.

He's gutted that he's not modelling for Gap, so I have to remind him how much he enjoyed doing his photo shoot. Likewise, he was disappointed not to win a heap of books when we spent the best part of a weekend turning a cardboard box into a Noddy car (word of advice: if you run out of poster paint, don't let the kids loose with emulsion tester pots instead) – but he was so proud of his work that he asked to do it again just a few weeks later. The video we made for an Oreo comp was an even greater success, although since that involved eating biscuits, perhaps there's no surprise there.

The short of it is, there's no point comping with children if they don't enjoy the process. Of course, you could always say the same for adults. For example, that comping is a crutch for my mental health is no secret. However, were I to find myself stressing about deadlines and losing sleep in order to squeeze in those last few entries at the end of the day/week/month or whatever, then clearly my hobby would no longer be fit for purpose.

Fortunately, that's not really an issue for me. Indeed, I generally have only to think about my reasons for comping and that's motivation enough to complete a session: I enter comps to win quality time with my wife and to make my kids happier at Christmas.

What I don't do, however, is comp for the cat. I've enough ingratitude in my life already.

Luck

Fortune is where you find it – often enough, it's just a case of knowing where to look. For example, about 150 yards from where I live there's a house with a hazelnut tree. Clearly, the owner gets his fill of nuts because, come autumn, you can grab a pocket-full off the path every time you pass.

Why people ignore this manna is anyone's guess. Me, I roast them, freeze them and trough at leisure.

And when this little harvest season passes, it's chestnut time – which generally entails a good stamp around the copse down the road. It's also about this time that I start bulking up for winter, as there's little to beat roast chestnuts and hot chocolate when you have (or at least, your kids think you have) spent too long in the fresh but chilly autumn air.

For most people, of course, gathering nuts does not fall under the umbrella of prize-winning. I'd have to agree. My point is simply that it's important to celebrate good fortune.

It's also important to recognise that fortune is out of your hands; that fortune is the hand you are dealt.

Luck, by contrast, is more than just favourable circumstances – it's about leveraging those circumstances to make something happen. The phrase, 'knowing my luck', has long since disappeared from my vocabulary: if I'm not in the process of being lucky, it's because I'm scanning the horizon for the opportunity to be lucky.

For example, when my son lost his first tooth, he convinced himself that the Tooth Fairy was going to give him a fiver for it. No amount reasoning would disabuse him of this notion. For this reason, I wrote him a letter from the Tooth Fairy setting out her tariff, snapped it quickly, and popped it on Facebook to give my family a laugh. A week later, my post had had 4000 shares. Heart Radio had also got on it and posted the letter on their various local Facebook pages, so it had a few thousand more shares too. As Andy Warhol would no doubt have said, everyone goes viral once.

While this was blowing up, I wondered if there was any way of leveraging the situation to my advantage, and so brought it to the attention of Brush-Baby, the children's toothcare company. They liked it so much that they gave us a review kit of their various electric toothbrushes and toothpastes. I hadn't entered any competition, and yet it felt just like winning.

That's when it dawned on me that making your luck is not just about looking for those competitions with the best odds – the local, effort-based, or simply badly promoted. Sometimes it involves conjuring competitions out of thin air. Competitions with no other entrants and no closing dates. No terms, no conditions, and, to be brutally honest, no guaranteed prizes either.

OK, so not technically competitions then, but semantics has never been my strong point. The point is, when everything goes to plan, the result is an experience that most definitely feels like winning.

Unless someone has a better idea, I'm calling this karmic comping. Why karmic? Because goodwill generates goodwill.

To be sure, it isn't for everyone. Cynics, in particular, might want to skip past this bit, because without genuine charm and brand affection, it absolutely will not work. This is another reason why I try to rope my children into my videos – while I commonly feel surly and beat, if I give my lads free rein, they are ripe with spontaneous (and often ill-informed) sincerity.

Case in point: for some months, my eldest lad's most prized possession was a purple Pilot Frixion pen. He loved that pen. No toy came close. So I made a video about him and his purple pen of power. And then I sent it to Pilot.

They loved it. They shared it. And they sent my delighted son another four of their fancy Frixion pens.

So what's the lesson here? Brands love to share user-generated content because it's genuine, grassroots love. It shows how their product makes a difference to real people. In turn, people connect with it, because it's completely shorn of corporatism.

In other words, if you love a brand then let them know. And if you can let them know in a way that tickles their chestnuts, who knows ... maybe they'll love you back. That's karma.

Mojo

'But how do you stay positive when you're not winning?'

Year in, year out, this remains the number one question people ask me (although 'who does your hair?' and 'can I see your licence?' do rank pretty high). The bottom line, of course, is that I put so much effort into worrying about the heavy stuff, like my children's happiness, my job satisfaction and why the cat is making so much noise, that it's genuinely difficult to accommodate any more negativity in my head. Plus I'm so well practised at not winning that I generally forget to notice. But all that's a question of personal temperament. More objectively, the important thing to remember is that no one wins all the time. Even world-class compers have dry spells. Their droughts are probably shorter, but everything is relative. The important thing is to maintain a positive outlook.

Naturally, that's easier said than done. And what works for one person may not work for another. For instance, some people have a portfolio of motivational mantras. That's not really my bag, though I would agree that:

- the dictionary is the only place where quitting comes before winning; and

- winners are just losers who don't give up.

Some folks, meanwhile, put great stock in karma. Dismiss this as hokey superstition if you will, but first take a moment to dress it differently. Call it community. Invest in it and the returns will come with interest. Find yourself some comping buddies. If you see comps local to them, or with prizes you know they want, or effort-based comps that play to their strengths, then let them know. Doing good feels good. What's more, the favours will be returned. Support will be reciprocated. Karma by any other name would smell so sweet.

But what if you need something more empirical? When I need to feel lucky, I just remind myself that I *am* lucky. I've a number of ways of doing this, but mostly they boil down to the same thing: celebrating previous wins.

The most basic method involves digging out my spreadsheet of wins in order to bask in the glare of cold, hard facts. In this respect, there are two main ways to consider the data: frequency and bottom line.

Bottom line is great. In the UK, at the very least, that's your tax-free haul. Cool stuff you haven't paid for. If you've had a few big-ticket wins, it makes even better reading.

My bottom line tends not to be outstanding. That's not to say I'm unhappy with it – on the contrary, it's a very reasonable conversion rate given how little effort I make compared with some people. But what really works for me is my win frequency. No matter how many people call me a winner, I never get bored of it.

Nevertheless, all this is just numbers.

Personally, I'm a big fan of photographing my wins as they roll in so I can look back on the good times whenever the inevitable dry season rears its sorry head. What's more, the dry season provides a perfect opportunity to dust the virtual trophy cabinet, whether that entails hashtagging those wins on Instagram or curating a winspiration board of prizes on Pinterest.

Mostly, my prizes come in drips and drabs, so I can only really snap them one at a time. In terms of win frequency, however, December 2017, was my most successful month ever – in fact, things went so well that the goodies were literally stacking up faster than I could find homes for them. And that's when I remembered prize piles.

When I first started comping, I used to pore slack-jawed over the winners' stories on PrizeFinder, gasping at the heaps of things some people were winning on a monthly basis. And I thought: one day, this will be me. And so it was – I was living the dream!

Dry spells are an inevitable part of comping, so when I realised that this beautiful moment was unfolding before me, I captured it, intending full well to use it in my next trip to the luck recovery clinic.

When I look back on this picture now, I think, 'Yes! I really can do this!' I may not be able to make an actual pile in any given month (read, most months), but I'm a total advocate for snapping every last win for posterity. Sure, the prize spreadsheet is great, but Kodak moments definitely resonate on a more emotional level.

If I need a more tactile way to feel lucky, however, nothing beats literally getting up close and personal with my prizes.

Consider, for example, the watch I won. Or watches, I should say. Fancy watches. His and hers fancy watches. They're made by Mr Jones Watches, and they're utterly crackers.

Hand-made in London with a self-winding mechanism, these are bona fide timeless masterpieces, which is to say, they not only lack numbers, but also any hands.

The last time I had to consult the instructions for a wristwatch I was six. In that respect, this win has given me an exquisitely novel way to relive my childhood that doesn't entail wrestling with the hourly chime on a plastic Casio.

While it's not the first time someone has designed a timepiece without the conventional indicators, this has to be one of the most bonkersest designs yet. It's like someone copped a snook at the entire history of timekeeping and thought, nah – I've got a much better idea.

I'm going to level with you here: it's not a practical solution. If you're the type of person who keeps time through quick, furtive glances at their watch, then you'd hate them.

On the other hand, if you want a wrist ornament that demands contemplation before it yields the vaguest insight into matters horological, then these watches are the stuff of dreams.

Every time I don my watch, I think, 'that's my lucky watch'. It's the perfect piece to accessorise my lucky tee-shirt and my lucky hoodie. Heck, I've even got lucky pants, for when things really get tough. In short, when I need a pep, I dress lucky. It doesn't matter if those wins don't coordinate, or if it means wearing six socks to go down the Co-op, because I am literally dressed as a winner.

While I'm at it, I dig out any vouchers I've won but not yet redeemed and make time to remember the good times.

The £300 Virgin Experiences voucher I won came at such a time. A sensible person might have spent some time browsing the catalogue, as it were. Not me. In about the time it took to write that last sentence, I'd blown it on a spa break. In my day-to-day life, I waste hours deliberating over the merits of Decision A versus Decision B; not this time, however – I just went arrow-straight to the nearest place with chips and a dressing-gown dress code.

That place was Clarice House, in Bury St Edmunds, and I booked the break to coincide with my 15th wedding anniversary. Given that we hadn't so much as grabbed a pint to celebrate any anniversary since the delivery of our first-born in 2010, I figured that back rubs and jacuzzis would make a pleasant change. (Here I should add that the package also included unlimited use of the hotel gym, though why anyone would entertain an exercise bike when they could spend the day in a fizzy bath escapes me.)

So, after half a year of waiting, the day finally came. We bundled the children off to my mum's house, fired up the Astra, and broke down 20 minutes away from home.

The RAC promised to arrive within three hours (three!). Such faint reassurance invariably puts my stress into fifth gear, and indeed, for the next 90 minutes there was a bona fide risk that my anxiety would boil into a violent but ultimately pointless assault on my vehicle; that or vomiting on the grass verge. I try not to be a control freak, but I had seen the day going differently. Thankfully, the hotel was sympathetic, and rescheduled the treatments for later that day.

In the end, we lost only two hours of R&R. Small mercies, I suppose, but my state of mind was plain to see, even by the time we arrived at the hotel another hour later. Indeed, two hours of pool, jacuzzi and steam room made barely a dent on the residual tension, as evidenced by the therapist's unrestrained awe vis-à-vis the incredible gnarl of my shoulders (largely accumulated since I last relaxed, some time in October 2016).

The back rub, however, was one of the most effective of my life – I wince to recall just how much lactic acid was released from my knotted muscles. Judging from the way I stumbled out of the treatment room like a zombie on mogadon, it seemed pretty clear that those toxins were the only thing holding my body together. I collapsed in the relaxation room until reality came back into focus.

Regrettably, that was a little quicker than I would have liked, if only because of the piped music. I'm clearly the minority, but I'd rather listen to extra-mild cheddar than the emotionally vacant tedium of so-called 'relaxing music' – there's more soul in a tape full of ZX Spectrum games. So I schlepped back up to our room and sat in the vast bathtub until it was time to eat.

At the risk of dwelling on things not going to plan, dinner didn't start by going to plan. That was because we were given a complimentary bottle of prosecco, however, so I can let that stand – everything goes better with bubbles, after all.

As it was only a few pounds more, we upgraded to the perfectly cooked and deceptively large steak meal. I say deceptive because, as a doltish bumpkin, I am unaccustomed to eating from rectangular platters, and before I knew it, had over-eaten. I then compounded the matter by shoving down a humungous crème brulée.

Good times did not ensue. My belly threw its rattle from the pram, and I spent the rest of the night feeling horribly ill until, by the grace of God, I fell unconscious. Indeed, it wasn't for another two days that I could eat anything without feeling like I'd ingested cast iron. Again, this wasn't high on my list of objectives for the break.

Nevertheless, when dawn came with rosy fingers, I felt many times better than the night before. Perhaps not man enough for the full English, but sufficiently strong for eggs royale and a sneaky pain au chocolat before the digestive predicament came to light.

We also had full use of the facilities again, so a lie-down in the relaxation room (this time with suitable distractions) was just what the doctor ordered. That and another hour and a half in the jacuzzi and steam room.

Sadly, of course, all good things must come to an end, and so we loaded up the motor and promptly ducked back inside to order lunch, which we ate on the terrace, and followed up with a leisurely walk around the grounds. Well, my counsellor did tell me to spend more time enjoying the moment...

Novelty

Raindrops and roses and whiskers on kittens. That's the last time you'll hear me mention them in the same breath as like-share and follow-retweet comps. I'm not saying I'm above either, but as entry mechanics go, they're not only braindead, but also require literally zero interaction with the brand.

Why is this so important? Because if promoters don't create the right kind of buzz around a brand, they're focusing their marketing effort on garnering short-term interest that'll be forgotten as soon as the page is closed – and the brand with it.

Sure, the winners are going to get a warm fuzzy feeling every time they hear the promoter's name, but who else? Imagine you're desperate for a PS4, and in the last six months entered every last competition to win one – how many of those promoters can you still name, and how many have been lost in the general haze swirling round your head?

Are comps with lots of smaller prizes any better? Certainly, the physical footprint of the promotion is larger as more people will be touched personally by the brand, and their affection for said brand will flourish accordingly. But again, what about the folks who go without? What impact has the promoter's marketing (for that is what the competition is, after all) had on them?

For some promoters, this is simply the price of harvesting contact details for a future mailshot. They've done the maths, and they're happy with that. Promoters looking for something more touchy-feely, however, such as raising brand awareness or improving customer relationships, may well be disappointed.

That's why I enjoy the novelty of creative competitions, especially those that oblige entrants not just to make an effort, but actually to immerse themselves in the brand.

That probably sounds a bit poncey, so let me give a few examples.

First, consider the Human Centipede. I've little positive to say about this nauseating franchise, but when the DVD of the last movie was released, I had to applaud the promoters for going the extra mile. That they were giving away the DVD was no surprise. The marquee prize, meanwhile, was a dirty great gogglebox – a great thing in itself, but as prizes go, not really fizzing with originality. Where the promoters excelled, however, was the entry mechanism. No one was accepted into the draw without first submitting a photograph of themselves on their hands and knees. Why? So the promoter could photoshop them into a giant centipede.

Distasteful? Certainly. But absolutely relevant to the movie; absolutely memorable; and absolutely the only time an entry mechanic has required anyone to have their mouth digitally stitched onto a complete stranger's anus.

Another campaign I enjoyed was back in 2014 and was run by Hafele, the furniture fittings and architectural hardware company. This was a two-part campaign to raise brand awareness by getting people to talk about the brand, or more specifically, to pronounce its name.

It was a simple conceit – record yourself saying 'Hafele' and upload it to the company's Facebook page. Every entrant was then sent a branded t-shirt and asked to tweet a picture of themselves wearing it in order to be entered into a sweepstakes for £5,000, with something like 50 electric drills for runners-up. Power tools, I concede, aren't everyone's bag, but £5,000 is quite some draw.

In a matter of weeks, two of the biggest social media platforms were swimming in pictures and videos about Hafele. And in case you're wondering how it's pronounced, the promoter didn't actually care, as long as you were talking about them.

More simple, but of equal genius was a competition from PayPal to leverage its 'New Money' marketing campaign.

Here, it's worth bearing in mind that a key aim of advertising is to strengthen brand associations through well-timed repetition. In this instance, the promotion pounced on a topical event – the withdrawal of the paper five-pound note in 2017.

The precision timing of the competition was textbook: the old five pound note ceased to be legal tender on Friday, 6th May and the competition ran on the following Monday, with the catchline, 'New money doesn't expire' – a great example of using a competition to reinforce the campaign message.

Second, advertising with an emotional message, rather than a rational one, has a greater impact on customer attention, memory and behaviour. Here, the competition targeted frustrated members of the public who had just missed the window of opportunity for spending their paper money and gave them the chance to add a silver lining to their cloud. In other words, PayPal offered to make a virtue out of their fail. That kind of touchy-feely stuff generates positive brand sentiment by the gallon.

Third, a hundred people won a tenner's worth of PayPal credit – that's a great prize pot by any measure.

Fourth, to redeem the prize, the winners had to log in to their PayPal account, which is to say, they had to experience the brand – the positive emotion associated with their win combining with the familiar visual elements of the brand to create the best possible impression on their long-term memory.

Winners without a PayPal account of course needed to set up one tout suite – another win for PayPal, as all marketers like to grow market share.

It's the originality of competitions like these that really makes me smile because they help keep the hobby fresh. The truth is, I won nothing in the Hafele draw, and I didn't even enter the Human Caterpillar comp (for logistical rather than moral reasons), but because of the engagement factor, these campaigns are indelibly imprinted onto my mind – such is the power of awesome promotion.

Oh

Not everyone is on the same wavelength, are they?

Take pie, for example. I love pie. I entered a competition to win pie. I won pie. Then I won even more pie. Well, technically, on both occasions I won vouchers for pie, which is even better, as it's basically pie cash. Plus it would have been physically impossible for me to store such an obscene volume of pie.

As a pie-winning veteran then, the next time I won pie, I rather expected the promoter would find a similar solution for uniting me and the prize pie. What I did not expect was for a fresh meat pie to turn up a few days later. Certainly not a fresh meat pie that had spent the weekend in a courier's warehouse without an ice pack. In June. Possibly I'm a bit precious, but I didn't eat it. Did I mention it was also a day past its use-by date? Maybe it was ornamental pie.

I've also won milk – eight pints of it – again sent by courier.

It's not that the prize came out of the blue – I knew I'd won milk. But what I was expecting was a voucher or two – not a hamper of moo juice; not £3 worth of perishable goods sent by courier. How much that milk would have cost to send I couldn't say, but I do know that if you need a rich tea biscuit by this time tomorrow, the Royal Mail will dock you the best part of a tenner.

An isolated incident? Not at all. One summer, a promoter sent me 750 grams of salt. Cost of delivery? Nearly three times the value of the prize.

Yes, I do live in Norwich. But despite what you might have read, we do have supermarkets. And those supermarkets do accept vouchers.

So what's going on here?

My old economics tutor would have had one thing to say: follow the money.

A paper trail like this can mean only one thing: black ops couriers. By targeting FMCG firms, they're diverting a steady dollar stream to their employers without raising suspicion. It's embezzlement in plain sight, laundered and legit. There are whole syndicates of them – Google it – pooling their intelligence and planting moles in companies with cheap, heavy goods.

Go on, call me crazy – but, come Jersey Royal season, people are literally winning potatoes. Likewise, the Ice Company's giveaways involve mailing out ice. Ice! During the last World Cup, one lucky comper won a dozen bags of the stuff! Well, technically she received four, as eight had completely melted, while one had leaked all over the courier's van.

That prize may have been a washout, but at least it yielded some pleasure, unlike the time I won football tickets from a super low-entry competition to watch Norwich City play. Sure, it was only a pre-season friendly, but it was Premier League opposition – a perfect opportunity for my first-born to see his first match.

Bums on seats is clearly an issue for friendlies: two days later, I found a second competition. This time the shirt sponsor was giving away 250 pairs of tickets to the game.

It was a sign: one giveaway with barely a dozen entrants, and another with an absurd number of prizes – surely I could score a winner?

What I failed to account for, however, was my summer itinerary.

The summer itinerary is something that happens *to* me every year.

The process unfolds as follows: the school year finishes and my wife places a calendar in front of me;

my eyes glaze over, and an hour later, the next six weekends have vanished in a haze of ink and sighs.

Oh well, I thought. Good feeling or no, planning one's life around wins that are yet to materialise is the cornerstone of a gambling problem. And so, without another thought, I consigned my little jolly to the trashcan.

Two days later, I received a winning e-mail from the first promoter: Congratulations! You've won three tickets to the match!

I sighed, and asked them to redraw – the first time in my life that I've ever had to decline a prize.

And wouldn't you know – the second time was just around the corner. Adding insult to injury, I won another two tickets to the game – giving the declined prize a grand value of £50.

It just goes to show that some you win, and some you lose. And sometimes, clearly, you do both.

Purchase necessary

For a number of reasons, I've historically steered clear of purchase-necessary competitions, not least because I get most of my groceries delivered and I can't trust Tony Tesco to pick the right products. I'm also reluctant to stuff my face with deep-fried calorie-dense junk on the off-chance of winning a tote bag.

Come the summer of 2018, however, I realised that I was comping myself into a corner. It's easily done, of course. When your only opportunity to comp is on the lav or in the two minutes before school while the children are wrestling with their shoelaces and/or each other, you reach for the easiest option – in my case, Instagram.

And for a while, it was working. By the middle of the year, I had averaged one Insta win a week – better than the rest of my endeavours combined. But nothing lasts forever. As Instagram became a more fertile source of giveaways, so my fortune declined. Maybe that was due to the rise of the infinite-entry comp, or maybe more comps are being run across platforms. Then again, maybe seagulls follow the trawler because they think sardines will be thrown into the sea.

The only thing anyone can know for sure is that it's more useful to do different than dwell. For this reason, I stumbled out of my comfort zone, and had a good sniff of the purchase-necessary comps.

What I found here is that not all purchase comps are created equal. For a start, there's a major difference between a comp that wants a unique code and one that wants a batch code and one that wants a barcode. Last year, my Anchor Butter barcode scored a lunch-bag on the second attempt, while my Dairylea Dunkers' barcode got more play than Daniel Sturridge – and definitely won more. Likewise, the batch code on the discarded Pepsi Max bottle I found on my mindfulness course probably had a greater impact on my mental health than the class itself.

As for the unique codes … well, that's not exactly where my luck runneth over. My track record is brief: two plushies. These were given away by Plenty in a promotion that its marketing agency promised would 'really inject some fun and excitement into the Household Towel category, not only by adding value with every pack, but also through recruiting younger families into the category and ultimately driving incremental volume'.

So, I might not have won big, but when it comes to fun and excitement in the Household Towel category, you really can't put a price on those memories.

Of course, it's one thing to buy an alternative brand of loo roll when the competition packs are on special, but it's quite another to neck a jerrycan of Powerthirst in the hope of scoring anything better than Type 2 diabetes. But each to his own. Personally, I'd love to win an Xbox from Lucozade, but having imposed a four-penny ceiling on how much I'm willing to pay for a bottle, the eggs in my basket are strictly wombled, which is to say, grubbily plucked from the public highway. (NB When it comes to gaming the system with purchase-necessary competitions, there is, inevitably, a line in the sand. For the absence of doubt: wombling Lucozade bottles is perfectly acceptable; stealing McDonald's Monopoly stickers at knifepoint – as happened in West London back in 2018 – is not.)

If my mum only knew how much litter I've trousered she'd hit the roof. Or possibly the gin. Either way, she'd be sobbing about where on earth she went wrong.

She may have a point. I spent my 42nd birthday arm-deep in the local nursery's waste bin, trying to retrieve the Lucozade bottle I'd recklessly binned before checking the entry mechanic. And I did walk my six-year old son round the McDonald's car park looking for Monopoly properties. And yes, that was me sheepishly hiding an empty cider bottle behind my back when my son's head teacher collared me one morning before school.

But what matters dignity when there's gold at the end of that rainbow?

To be fair, I'm not sure a Big Mac Meal and a McFlurry count as gold, but at least they won temporary adoration from my first-born without compromising my principles about letting Ronald McDonald get his greasy fingers on my hard-earned cash.

Why I have these arbitrary principles is beyond me. My father insisted I got my stubbornness from my mum, although I'm pretty sure I get it from my son. In any case, my bloody mindedness invariably serves only to spite myself. Consider, for example, the Walker's Snap & Share comp from 2017. All I needed was one bag – one! – and I could have been off to watch Champions League football or playing Pro Evolution Soccer on one of the five hundred PlayStation 4 consoles being given away. Instead, I obstinately waited to womble a packet, by which time there was about a fortnight left to enter. Sure, I won an adidas football (by far the finest of the various balls I've won in my time – and certainly classier than the one signed by a bunch of Screwfix shills whose sole claim to fame was sharing a name with a former England player), but imagine if I'd pulled my pointlessly principled finger out?!

Here, I can only paraphrase Beverly Knight: what-ifs are for chumps. The only sensible thing to do is to take your ball home and move on – something that's never hard when there's a glut of prize-heavy instant win promotions, such as there was through the summer of 2018.

The most obvious example was the Ribena Pick Your Own Gig promotion, through which my wife and I were blessed with more than a dozen bottles of Ribena and a few quids' worth of Amazon vouchers. To be sure, I missed out on the biggies, but scoring soft drinks is always handy in summer.

Most people would agree that the Ribena comp was considerably more generous than the ongoing Lucozade Made to Move promotion that I entered religiously for more than two years and won only the lowest-tier prize, twice. I say 'won' but the 'free bottle of Lucozade' came in the form of a voucher that I had a fortnight to redeem and wasn't accepted at any major supermarket. It also didn't cover the full cost of the product, so for two years running it has cost me fourpence to purchase my prize. And I don't even like Lucozade.

But I digress. More important is the fact that I'm a terrible sleeper. At best, I'll wake up some time around 3 am and then some time annoyingly close to my wife's alarm going off, then again when the alarm actually goes off, and again when she actually gets out of bed. Come the weekend, the alarm clock gets put on ice for a couple of days so that the children can wake me up at a similar time instead. Weeknights, my wife will still be working by the time I go to bed, so the odds of me waking up when she turns in are pretty good too. On top of this, one of our children recently had a season of wee-hour nosebleeds and bed-wetting during which sleeping was strictly off the menu. And did I mention the banging and gurgling of the central heating? Yeah, that and all.

Poor sleep patterns are universally annoying, and yet for the comper, slightly interesting too. That's because the prizes in many 'instant win' competitions become available during 'winning moments' – in other words, the chance of winning depends on the time you enter.

The prevailing wisdom is that there are good times to enter, and there are bad. Bad is the peak time – daytime, especially lunchtime and other down times; good – at least for competitions open 24 hours a day – is when anyone in their right mind is asleep. And since sleep deprivation has been a deadweight on my comping, I figured it was about time for it to up its game. To this end, I decided to try small-hour comping.

For the first month or so, my success was limited to the Walkers/Pepsi Perfect Match promotion, from which I won a plastic bowl and a couple of tumblers, one of which had been smashed in the mail. To be sure, wins on this scale fall under the umbrella of tiny acorn rather than great oak; however (and more importantly), they also bear out the theory that moonlight comping can indeed bring grist to the mill.

But why settle for grist when bigger fish are just crying out to be fried? The Freddo's Big Adventure and Dairylea Super Cool or Super Cheesy promotions were two such fish. Generous, lovely fish that were happy for folks to paste in the same barcode for their every entry. This was great because I could copy the code to my phone's clipboard before going to bed, thus minimising the fat-finger foul-ups I typically make when trying to complete entry forms with my eyes shut.

Shining blue light into my face when I should have been KO took about a week to pay dividends: Freddo ponied up GoApe tickets, while the benevolently bonkers gods of Dairylea blessed me with a Polaroid instant print camera, which due to some clearly categorical error they had classified as a cheesy prize, lumping it in with the karaoke kits and branded onesies.

Obviously, I mean no disrespect to Dairylea, but giving away 150 cameras on top of 100 Samsung tablets, 100 Bose speakers and 100 bikes is definitely bonkers. On top of this – unlike with the Freddo or, for that matter, Foster's Thirstiest Place on Earth comps that were running concurrently – the Dairylea T&C didn't initially restrict the number of times people could enter each day. Unsurprisingly, it didn't take long for a cottage industry of cheese-wielding cut-and-pasters to spring up and tap away 24/7 in the hope of bagging a giant Jenga set. If memory serves, one person managed 7000 entries before being politely asked to cease, desist, and perhaps let someone else have a go.

To any insomniac whose eyes are lighting up on reading this, I must mention one thing: much like the house creaks so much louder at night, so too is the winning buzz amplified. If you're fortunate enough to get a shot of that sweet dopamine-adrenaline combo when the larks are still knocking out zeds, then you might want to chase it down with some Night Nurse, as grabbing shut-eye when you're still high on victory is easier said than done. So far, two of my nights have been a write-off, suggesting that I'd be much better entering at 4 am than 2. Whether that would be a good time in terms of winning moments, however, who knows? I've successfully Shazammed a Foster's can at 5 am, but that's scarcely enough data to establish a pattern.

I've also had one instance of success with Peperami, but keying in those absurdly long unique codes is an utter pig as the website won't let you paste them in. That's not to say it isn't worth also saving those codes to your phone – the wrappers are hard enough to read in the daylight, and it takes only a small stash on the bedside table to fragrance the whole room with delicate porky musk.

While I have every intention of continuing this bleary-eyed endeavour, the question remains: what price a good night's sleep? For a £150 camera, I'm happy to spend the next day as a crotchety growl-bag. The only thing is, in my twilight stupor I thought I'd won something else – a (genuinely cheesy) disposable camera. Not something that most people would toss and turn the rest of the night over. But then again, maybe people should take more pleasure from not being on the wrong side of a four-penny mugging.

Quidditch

Ten months after winning tickets to the Harry Potter tour, I finally booked our trip. That's right, ten months later. I hadn't planned to sit on it for so long, but here's the thing: you can't just rock up at the Warner Bros Studios and expect to be let in. And if it's a school holiday trip you're after, patience is not so much a virtue as a prerequisite.

I work freelance, and the very the nature of my work (or perhaps just my client) is so very last-minute that it's impossible to say when a quiet spell will be upon me. This makes it hard to forecast my schedule for the next day, never mind six months ahead, like most people seem to be able to manage for this experience.

The other thing is that my lads are still small. At the point that I won the tickets, my oldest was having nightmares about Willy Wonka, while the youngest was hiding under the sofa cushions whenever Dobby the house elf stepped on screen – so much for the comic relief. With this in mind, I figured there was every chance that they might take the gloss off the experience.

For this reason, we waited about as long as we could before booking our visit, in the hope that they might man up a little. Unfortunately, we still never made it past the Chamber of Secrets.

Not to be beaten, we thought we'd make the trip as straightforward as possible by staying nearby, so that we could arrive first thing, without the stress of driving two volatile delinquents across country. As the experience of driving to the spa break I won previously still loomed large in my mind, I was also anxious not to involve the RAC in our lives any more than strictly necessary.

While the prize didn't include travel or lodging expenses, I figured that this additional outlay would be an investment in happiness – after all, what child doesn't enjoy the novelty of a naff pub dinner and a night in a hotel?

What I didn't budget for was the four year-old going on a rampage and refusing to sleep till 10. The other one wasn't much better. As I sat in a dark Travelodge room, drinking whisky from the toothbrush mug while my cold-ridden wife snored, I reflected on how I'd envisaged the evening going differently.

The next morning, as you might have guessed, the youngest lad was so exhausted that his monstrous screaming fits recurred with the tedious inevitability of the post-Christmas credit card bill. Given also that I was a few weeks into the stress and blues of a heinous work bender, the day ahead was never going to be easy.

Getting to the Warner Bros Studios was a piece of cake. Getting inside was something else.

First we queued to get the tickets. This queue was short but painfully slow, as the dispensing machine was woefully inept. It was also a waste of time as I was unable to provide the telephone number that the promoter had used when booking the tickets, so the machine refused to recognise me.

As such, I joined the longer queue so I could chat with the counter staff. By this point, the antisocial behaviour of my eldest was at peak malevolence, so my wife removed both children from my line of sight.

After this queue, we joined the queue for bag checks. Finally, we joined the queue to get in.

Let's just say it was a very British experience.

Nevertheless, we were now in, and the excitement could begin…

Of all the queues, the one to actually commence the tour was the largest and most densely packed. It would probably have been less stressful had my children been on reins, so I will bear that in mind for future reference. That said, as the numbers built up, the oppressive hubbub worked wonders for intimidating them into line, and it was only another twenty minutes or so before we were in the Great Hall.

Many words come to mind on entering this cavernous space, but I'll settle for 'Gosh'. The room is so big that I'd always assumed it was shot on location. Well, you know what they say about assumptions. In an ideal world, I'd illustrate the vastness of the set with an awesome photo, but sadly my camera was giving me lip and I was unable to diagnose the problem while my spawn ran pell-mell about the place. Also, we had only about five minutes to take it all in, so by the time the children were contained, everyone was being booted out. In short, you'll just have to take my word for it: gosh, indeed.

Next was the hangar full of props. Oh my. I can't remotely do this justice. It's not just costumes and wands in here, but rooms – whole rooms – like Harry's dorm, the Griffyndor common room, Professor Umbridge's office, the Weasley kitchen, and the potions classroom, with the forbidden forest and Platform 9 3/4 just around the corner (along with the Hogwarts Express). You've also got a first-hand introduction to the special effects in here – and not some basic show-and-tell affair either. You want to sit at Hagrid's table or summon a broomstick? No problem. Heck, you can even buy a video of yourself riding that broomstick or sitting on the Hogwarts Express as it gets attacked by dementors – though you might want a word with your bank manager first, given that photos were, at the time of writing, going for about £14 a pop while video footage was £25 a clip.

I didn't mention the wand fighting lessons did I? Well, you'll need them later on when you're duelling with death eaters on the Hogwarts Bridge. In my case though, my kids were more interested in Hagrid's motorbike and the flying car from the second movie, which were parked nearby, so the ten inches of wooden dowel I was waving around like a prat was purely for my own benefit.

It's about this point that refreshments are called for. Given that the Warner Bros Studio is one of possibly four places in the world where one can buy butterbeer, we made a point of grabbing ourselves a beaker each. Which is to say, the grown-ups got one each while the boys got to bear witness. They have only themselves to blame, of course: given their longstanding aversion to new flavours, I'm disinclined to stump up £6.50 for a half-pint of pop that's more likely to end up on the floor than in a belly. It's also worth noting that for that kind of price per litre, you could not only get a very reasonable prosecco, glass hire and change, you could forgo the remedial dentistry and all.

It was the right call – the children each had one sip of the horrifically calorific blend of butterscotch and cream soda and decided it wasn't for them. For future reference, I'd recommend the prosecco; however, if rotting your mouth is up there on your bucket list, I understand that the Flying Cauldron butterscotch beer available on Amazon is pretty similar.

Outside the refreshment area you can also have a nosey at the night bus and take a quick tour of the Dursleys' house (again – I can't believe this scenery was built for the movie – I honestly had to touch it to believe it). You're also only minutes away from the incredible Diagon Alley, but don't get ahead of yourself – there's all the CGI and robotic FX to take in first.

If, like me, your time in this zone is curtailed by one of your offspring having a tantrum while the other harasses the staff, the one thing you absolutely *must* experience is the bit where you get to control a fully-rendered animation of Dobby the house elf via real-time interactive motion capture. This is a once-in-a-lifetime opportunity to make Dobby floss, dab, or whatever else it takes to impress a child these days.

The penultimate area is dedicated to the set designers – the unsung heroes of the franchise – the folks who pretty much conceived the entire shebang. Their sketches offer a first-class insight into the production process and leave you in bona fide awe of their imagination.

Finally, it's time for the money shot: the absurdly intricate 1:24 scale model of Hogwarts. That translates to a model almost 50 feet in diameter. I really can't overstate the incredibleness of this structure – for reference, the man-hours put into building and reworking the model, if totalled, would exceed 74 years.

So, all that remains is to exit through the gift shop. Here's the sucker punch. Everything – but everything – is obscenely expensive. For example, the markup on relatively pedestrian pocket-money items, such as a pack of Top Trumps, is at least 50 per cent over the standard market rate for similar (but non-Potter) items. You want a magic wand? That'll be £35 please. Understandably, my son wanted a souvenir, but when a chocolate frog costs a month's pocket money, the world was hardly his oyster – a displeasure he made clear to more than one member of staff. Eventually, however, he settled on a pair of Harry Potter specs for £4 – of the quality you might expect from a Poundland fancy-dress kit, that – yes – also contained other plastic tat. But his red mist for acquisition was at least sated and we could move on.

While the gift shop may have been an otherworldly affair for all the wrong reasons, I find it hard to imagine I will ever experience a day more magical than this, and I totally recommend it to anyone with even the slightest interest in the Potterverse. If I'm honest, I'd probably counsel against taking small children – or, more specifically, my children – but even despite their best efforts, it was worth the wait.

More than that, though, the day provided an important reminder of why I must not surrender to the shell-shock of parenthood, and why I cannot live my life from the back seat. All too often, I become so focused on surviving that I forget to live – and when you'd rather curl up in a ball than go to one, that's a worry. If it hadn't have been for my hobby, I might never have seen this magic up close. Plainly, comping has forced me to get more out of life and for that I will be forever grateful.

Relativity

Lots of compers say that the big one is just around the corner ... but just how big is that biggie?

Personally, I concentrate hardest on the smaller, more frequent wins. It's not that I dislike big wins (for I am not a fool) but I do have a fondness for shorter odds, and shorter odds tend to be associated with smaller prizes. The stats certainly bear this out for me: nearly half my wins have a face value no greater than £10.

In the world of seasoned compers, this possibly marks me out as a part-timer. So be it. But it does mean I'm never blasé about £50 prizes, and if I'm lucky enough to score a £100 win, you'll find me chest-bumping the mirror and whooping like an immature ambulance. On the few occasions I've topped the ton, I've actually felt a little unwell, like I've just spent a half hour on the waltzer necking tequila and Tizer. I daren't imagine what would happen if I won a car, but I'm pretty sure it'd require a doctor.

In any case, the fact remains that for me, a £100 prize is exceptional. As such, I'd call it a biggie. However, if I was winning a prize of that size every week (let me imagine that for a second...) then no doubt my opinion would be different.

In short, 'big' is relative.

Does this mean the world needs an objective metric-style system for measuring prize size?

Certainly, we could always assign a bunch of adjectives to a vague set of boundaries, such as under £50 being 'modest' and over £1000 being 'jumbo', but it's all a bit arbitrary and far too hard to remember.

Would it work to call our wins 'nice'? You've won a pen? Nice. A luggage tag? Nice. A £100 watch? Ah, you're right, that is better. Have another 'i'. Niice. A £200 giftcard? Niiice. A cruise round the Caribbean with three grand spending money? On second thoughts, let's not go there – I'll only lose count.

Nonsensical metrics aside, is it even wise to go there? What good would it do?

It may well be human nature to understand things through the lens of comparison, but once we start taking a tape measure to other people's success, it's only a small step before we're benchmarking ourselves against someone else and trying to live our lives according to their standards. And frankly, who's got time to waste living someone else's life?

I've never won a holiday. Some people have won several. There could be any number of reasons for this disparity, but it doesn't mean that what success I have had has any less value: my wins make me happy – that's the only measure that matters.

That's not to say prize-winning is the only thing that blows my horn – for all I sometimes find happiness elusive, my life really isn't that hollow. Sometimes the soup needs salt, and sometimes the soup needs pepper. It's just a matter of finding the damn cruet. In this regard, the best starting point for anyone is to recognise their own unique achievements and judge them by their own unique criteria.

In my case, I've now won enough tote bags to carry one on each finger, so that's got to count for something, right?

Stubbornness

Sometimes I win. Sometimes I learn. And sometimes I do the same thing over and over again in the hope that things will turn out differently next time.

Some would call that the very definition of insanity. And sometimes they'd be right. Sometimes, however, it's less clear-cut.

Case in point: for three weeks in a row I used the same entry for Heart Radio's Faces for Florida promotion. After failing to pass muster on the first week, the likelihood of a subsequent win was slim to nil, but as I didn't have any better ideas, my only option was to hope the rest of the field had a bad day.

Fanciful thinking? Maybe so, but a long shot is better than no shot, as Steven Bradbury found in the 2002 Winter Olympics when everyone else in the 1000m speed skating final fell over, leaving him to collect the gold.

Unfortunately for me, in this instance, the other entrants blew me out of the water. But on the plus side, I don't have to worry about taking an explosive eight-year-old on a long-haul flight.

Then there was the time, about three years ago, when I tried to win a Weetabuddy. For the uninitiated, this recurring competition requires entrants to scatter fruit on their breakfast in a sufficiently artful manner that it looks like a face. I chose the path less travelled, and skewered fruit to my biscuit so it could stand up.

As luck would have it, the promoter was looking for balanced breakfasts rather than edible voodoo dolls, and my entry failed to make the grade. Not that I really minded – at that point I was in thrall to the comping monkey on my back, and entering every effort comp I could find, just for the craic.

But I kept the picture. It wasn't like it was well composed, or for that matter remotely clever. But I did love how perfectly it encapsulated the absurdity of comping – after all, who in their right mind would pin blueberries to their cereal just to win a fluffy Weetabix? And more to the point, why would anyone even want a fluffy Weetabix?

I can't answer that last question, but I do know that my mojo was wanting a boot up the jacksie towards the end of the year, and on a whim, I entered the competition again. With the same picture.

Common sense would suggest that having failed once, the picture would only flop again. But common sense can bite me. I won that fluffy Weetabix. And my second-born loves it. At long last, he can hug his favourite cereal – something I'll never manage with granola.

So, what's my point? Simple: stubbornness pays.

Tech

I'm a Luddite. Not on purpose, you understand – I just have certain issues. Issues that prevent me finding the brain space to stay abreast of modern technology. By 'certain issues', I of course mean 'my issue'; and by 'my issue', I'm generally referring to my first-born, who is so addicted to the sound of his own voice that moments of silence actually cause him pain. Six years have passed since my neural network last sparked and it's only thanks to muscle memory that I can still operate a light switch.

For this reason, I try to enter tech giveaways only when I have a clear idea of what I need. For example, when our personal video recorder went belly up, I pulled out the stops to win a replacement. Unfortunately, what I ended up with was an HD media streamer and a headache. Two years later I still have no idea what either is good for.

However, when I saw that Aviva was giving away a whole heap of Amazon Echo Dots, the lure of the odds got the better of me.

As you'll have guessed, I was one of the winners. The doohickey arrived at the end of the Christmas holidays; it then sat on the shelf for the next eight months, waiting for me to have a couple of hours free from work, chores or children to explore what it could do (and how).

My initial hopes were somewhat kyboshed, as I was rather hoping to use it as a wireless speaker – something that had been on my wishlist for some time. Unfortunately, being the slack-jawed yokel that I am, Bluetooth was somewhat beyond my ken at that point and I'd barely progressed past interrogating Alexa about forthcoming football fixtures and her ability to open the pod-bay doors when my brood arrived home from their jolly.

On learning that that the device was fully programmed to entertain his poppycock, my first-born squealed with glee. In truth, I was pretty chuffed too, and flushed with self-satisfaction, popped into the kitchen to brief my wife about our new electric babysitter.

The smug smile lasted a whole three minutes, after which first-born trotted in to provide an update. He'd started a subscription to Amazon Music Unlimited.

It turns out that all Echo devices are, by default, allowed to bill your credit card based on voice authorisation alone. This much I discovered not because Amazon sent immediate confirmation of my new subscription (this didn't arrive for another hour), but because I found the transcript of the conversation between my son and Alexa. When asked if he wanted to pay a monthly subscription fee of £3.99, his response was 'sure', and his word was bond.

The only trouble was, he never said that. Rather, when asked if he wanted to subscribe, he walked out of the room. I know this, because I (eventually) found the audio files. The system had heard some background noise and felt this was good enough to close the contract. So, now I not only have two children who hear only what they want to hear, but I also have a passive-aggressive POS terminal furnished with selective hearing and my credit card details.

As I write, it's 2019 and my brain has almost digested 2016, which means I've finally learned how to pair Bluetooth-enabled devices. Just in time too, as I've recently won wireless headphones. The noise-cancelling function doesn't mute my children quite as much as I was hoping, but at least I have some kind of sanctuary when my first-born hijacks the room in order to list his five favourite ways with potato.

More to the point, I'm finally able to offer my ears shelter-in-place without leaving the auditory blast area. This means I've started listening – actually listening – to music again. It's like finding a nugget of my soul down the back of the sofa. Surely an immense victory by anyone's standards?

Well, maybe. Just as I started getting back in the habit, the cans went Pop. Sproing. Or whatever noise you might imagine a piece of tech might make when it's sitting on your head and then bursts open for No Good Reason. I'm guessing they arrived with a hairline crack at one end of the headband, and that said crack eventually decided to go nuclear. But since I failed to QC them when they arrived, that's pure speculation. Whatever it was, it was a fault the promoter had never seen before. More importantly, it was also something the promoter was disinclined to fix or replace.

Their best offer was 25 per cent off a new pair. Normally, I'd lap up a discount like that. But when my experience of a product is that it self-combusts before it's had a dozen outings, I feel a little reticent to renew it. I guess my Luddism still needs a little work.

Upgrades

I hate buying razor blades. In terms of gender-based spending with a pleasure factor of zero, they're up there with tampons. These things should be on tap. Instead, we have to pay over the odds for such essentials because their marketing teams are giddily burning through corporate dollars carpet-bombing the countryside with menstruating sky-divers and trying to convince stubbly muppets that wiping their face with a sixteen-blade testosterone wand will make them look like David Beckham. Sometimes communism doesn't sound so bad.

But this is hardly the forum for debating the merits of the free market system. The point is, until the end of 2014, I was contentedly batting at my bristles with a twin-blade antique face cleaver. All that changed when I won a shaving subscription that delivered a 200 per cent increase in blades per inch.

The reduction in nicks and razor burn was great, but that smooth-face free-roll was never going to last forever. Six months later I was at a crossroads: pay more for a better shaving experience, or quite literally cut off my face to spite my face.

You see, there's a down side to comping: it develops tastes, creates needs.

Thanks to comping, I now know why people choose afternoon tea over a pasty, and why they drink loose-leaf milk oolong rather than Tetley.

As for confectionery, it wasn't so long ago that my idea of aspirational candy was a chocolate Matterhorn. That was back when duty-free shops the world over made like Fort Knox and stacked their king-size Toblerones like gold bullion, and Alan Partridge scarfed a lap-full while driving barefoot to Dundee. Without doubt, Toblerone was the acme of sophistication.

Years later, however, it had become a staple. Partly that's because I could get my fix at Poundland, and partly that's because I'd won a silly amount of increasingly fancy top-end chocolate, culminating in a monster great stack from Octo.

Clearly, this chocolate was made for posher folk than I. Consider, if you will, Exhibit A: a 100 g bar of raw white chocolate with salted pistachios and a retail price of £8.50. Translated into Toblerone, that kind of dough would score a kilo of chocolate with enough change for post-binge Bisodol.

You can probably see where I'm going with this – yep, it's one of those problems that gets little sympathy: I'm becoming a chocolate snob – worse, a cocoa bore. At one point I was so flushed with the stuff that I was sprinkling my morning porridge with goji berries coated in raw chocolate. To the outside observer, I must look like a right middle class ponce, but I can honestly swear that I wouldn't recognise a goji berry in a goji berry museum.

My first-world problem is by no means limited to sugar and spice. I recently won some serum – man serum, to be precise. I was planning to let my wife use it, but at her behest I gave it a go. Which is to say, at her behest and under her direction, as I had not the first clue what it was for or how it should be applied given that my skincare regime had never graduated beyond patching cracked fingers with whatever lotion was parked next to the sink.

After just a week of half-heartedly following her guidance, the dry, flaky bags under my eyes had recovered no end, and now as far as I can tell just look like regular bags. This is awesome progress – but given that childcare commitments mean I can work only part-time, the idea of coughing up a bullseye for another 30 ml of this elixir gives me the heebie jeebies.

That said, it could be worse. I also won a month's worth of la-di-da serum for my wife. It retails at £200, which in terms of sustainability presents a lifestyle choice between slightly smoother skin and feeding our children.

Suddenly, that Toblerone habit pales into insignificance.

Videos

Will video kill the tie-break comp? I don't know, but I do suspect the number of video-based competitions is going to increase over the next few years. Why? Because we have the technology.

For my part, that consists of no more than my phone and the video-editing software that came bundled with Windows, but given my level of technical competence, that's quite enough. Maybe I'll explore the free or modestly priced video editors out there when I've got my head around such basics as lighting and narrative. However, given the speed with which technology advances these days, there'll probably have been another quantum leap in technology by then, and who knows what will be happening in the world of comping.

The fact is, technology is changing the comping landscape. To state the obvious, there were no web-based comps before the internet, no follow-retweet comps before Twitter, and no selfie comps before the world and his dog had a phone with a front-facing camera.

Of course, today's front-facing cameras don't just take half-decent photos – they're also capable of capturing respectable video footage too – and things will only improve.

I'm not born-digital. Aside from berating retailers, I get little joy from Twitter. Likewise, Snapchat, with its vacuous filters and counterintuitive interface, has done nothing for me except pacify my children at weddings and funerals.

In short, I am, despite my best efforts, a 40-something technophobe, guilty of spawning children purely so I have someone to sync my iPod when I retire.

It really won't be long before today's children are playing with video editors like I played with Mini Munchman. Sure, they'll still have written assignments at school, but video-based assignments aren't going to be limited to drama and media studies lessons. Their media literacy is going to be all over ours. In other words, unless I put the time in now, by the time the millennial generation discover video comping, I won't even get a look-in.

For this reason, I now find any excuse to exercise my directorial skills, the most obvious being my prize unboxing videos.

Judging from the analytics, people seem to enjoy these far more than they do my writing. I'm guessing this is because there's something timeless about watching a grown man being outfoxed by parcel tape while a semi-literate camera hog undermines the last dregs of his parental authority. Amazingly, some people have even told me they find these videos inspirational. I can only assume that's because my incompetence makes them feel better about their own parenting skills.

That's fine by me – I'm in over my head the moment I roll out of bed. I'm just happy to have captured some kind of dynamic in the video, because if I can repeat that kind of storytelling in a competition video then it could just make the difference between being a winner or an also-ran.

By way of example, when I entered WD40's life-hacks competition, I remembered that I had some recent footage of my youngest lad apologising for some misdemeanour or other that I was able to weave into the video to give it a bit more spice.

The decision paid off – a few weeks later, a congratulatory message popped up on my screen while I was working. In addition to the branded merchandise and cycle maintenance kit, I'd won bikes – four

Diamondback mountain bikes – one for everyone in the family. And then – as if that wasn't more than enough – there was also a GoPro Hero 5 video camera.

I sat there slack-jawed. It wasn't so much butterflies in my belly as a twister of panicked bats. For the preceding few weeks, my wins had been infrequent and modest. And then this: a year's luck in one great dollop. I messaged back to check it wasn't an administrative error. Surely, they didn't mean *all* this prize was for me?

But they did. I'd just had my biggest ever win – by an enormous margin. Nice, with ever so many 'i's. The camera would have been a great prize on its own and together the bikes were definitely worth more than the long-suffering Astra.

To be sure, I would have been overjoyed to have won such a prize from the kind of sweepstake where every entrant is on an equal footing. However, when you're so personally invested in a competition entry, you feel much more control over your fortune. The win feels *earned*, and the feeling is so much sweeter.

The other great thing about video competitions is the simple fact that because they require more effort, they get fewer entrants – meaning better odds.

That's not to say that every video comp is worth entering. The 2017 South Park 'I am the Fart' competition, for example, sounded great on paper: break wind for the camera and win a trip to San Francisco (where your Bronx cheer would be made into 'the official in-game fart' for the latest South Park video game). Where the promotion hit a real bum note, however, was that the final shortlist was determined by public vote – a mechanic so flawed as to guarantee disappointing most of the people most of the time. Well, most of the comping community anyway.

How so? Because voting competitions invariably degenerate into popularity contests, with the prize going to the person with the most friends and family – that is, unless any vote-buying cheats choose to steal the spoils. Even in the event that everything is above board, it's a cert that someone will cry foul, fingers will be pointed and teeth will be gnashed. No one comes out of it well.

The simple truth is that asking for Joe Public's two-penneth is invariably a bad idea. There are many reasons why this should be so, but I'll settle for 124,109, that being the number of people who petitioned the Natural Environment Research Council to name their new polar research ship Boaty McBoatface. Of course, as we now all know, Boaty McBoatface does not mean Boaty McBoatface: the ship was named Sir Richard Attenborough – the fifth-placed suggestion, which took just 10,284 votes. Is it any wonder the Great British public has had enough of experts?

Winning

Compers are often asked what their best ever prize is. It sounds like a simple question, but for me it's deceptively complex. Even assuming I could remember my catalogue of wins on demand, I'm not sure it's possible to answer that question objectively. I'm not even sure I'd give the same answer from one day to the next or from one person to another.

To the non-comper, the monetary value of a prize is probably the most obvious way to measure its greatness. To me, however, that's just accountancy – and quack accountancy at that. Why? Well, for starters, list price and market price just aren't the same thing. To take an extreme example, if you sort the watches on Amazon by size of discount, you'll inevitably find at least one that, were you to pay the recommended retail price, would leave your wallet several hundred pounds lighter, but that is currently being offered with a 90 per cent discount.

A list price like that would put this watch on a par with your Raymond Weils and Tag Heuers. The thing is, genuine high-end watch brands don't do fire sales. Insane discounting like this is just smoke and mirrors marketing. In other words, using RRP as a proxy for awesomeness is a blunt instrument at best. It makes no allowance for aesthetics or utility or any other criteria that might be especially important to the individual.

Of course, you could always refer back to your win-list spreadsheet and grade every prize on a scale of 1–10 using whatever arbitrary criteria are most meaningful to you, but that would be a whole new level of nutbaggery.

And all this is before we even get to the 'money can't buy' experiences.

So, whenever I'm asked what I consider my best prize to be, I freeze like the proverbial spot-lit rodent. I'm regularly hamstrung by pointless pedantry, and in this case I can never move beyond 'best, how?'

For me, 'best' means most cherished, and my most cherished win is the iPhone 5 I won during my first summer of comping.

I didn't have a dozen wins under my belt at this point, and the first thing I remember on receiving the winning notification was a sudden burst of nausea, as if someone was going to undo my win (and indeed, to this day, I never feel like something has been truly won till I've unwrapped the parcel).

After that I was just giddily impatient. I was using an abysmal phone at the time and I hated it like you can't imagine. It was mediocre when I got it, and 18 months into my contract it was worse than unfit for purpose.

Now, I'm pretty sure the 'new' phone was a reconditioned model (the fact that the promoter was a phone repair company was a major clue) but I didn't care – from that point, every call I made, every text I sent, reminded me that I was a winner. Remember, this was still my early days of comping, so it was like getting dozens of pep talks a day. On top of all that, I was able to enter so many more photo competitions (my previous phone didn't even have a selfie cam) that the prize single-handedly pushed my comping game up a gear.

In short, the prize changed my life. It's not the most expensive thing I've won, but it made me a better person – if only because I was cursing less.

What made this prize so special then was the intangible benefits it brought with it. More than simply a phone, I had won an experience.

Experiences make fantastic prizes as the memories last so much longer than fast-moving consumer goods. The ultimate experience, of course, is one that money can't buy, such as a meet and greet with one of your heroes. While I've not won one of those, I have won my-money-can't-buy experiences. For example, I never realised how beyond my means Wimbledon was until I checked just recently. On the final Saturday, it costs £30 just to walk around the grounds. Sure, you might get lucky and see someone warming up on the outside courts, but if you want to see the ladies' final, a Centre Court ticket is £170 for the day. And, yes, tickets for the men's final cost even more. So, assuming I'd managed to get through the ballot system and procure tickets for me and my wife, I'd be £400 down before so much as sniffing a strawberry.

It also stands to reason that if you want to eat there, you're going to be forking out a small wedge. Sure, 'tis but £2.50 for a bowl of the aforementioned strawberries, but man cannot live on fruit alone – not when there's all that cucumber to consider, although at £8.50 a glass, sourcing your five-a-day solely from Pimms' garnish is unwise in more ways than one.

You can therefore imagine how I felt when Robinsons (yes, the squash people) told me I'd won VIP tickets to the 2018 ladies' final. You can also imagine my strangled squeals of drawn-out frustration that for the next hour the only person I was able to share this news with had no concept of SW19, never mind corporate hospitality, on account of being only four years old.

If you're thinking that this is unusually good fortune for me, you'd be right. I couldn't possibly say what something like this is worth, but if it's not the fanciest prize of my life, then it's surely a close second, and certainly the most amazing thing I've ever won from a tie-break comp.

A tie-breaker? No, I couldn't believe it either. In the preceding five years of comping, my track record with tie-breaks could be summarised as follows:

- a nice cake (I was the only entrant); and

- a hoodie from an online smut-monger (four entrants; three of whom failed to read the brief).

In the latter case, I was actually hoping to win the dressing gown, so even here I was wide of the mark.

Missing the mark is of course an area where it is incredibly easy to excel. In the present instance, for example, I drew a blank for three consecutive weeks before Robinsons took a shine to my suggestion for a new flavour for its Fruit Creations range.

Truthfully, I was never going to win in the first week – there were over a thousand entrants, and regardless of how tasty my idea might have been, I always knew that it lacked the mustard to stand out from such numbers. In Week 2, however, I pulled my socks up and tossed in a tennis pun or two.

Nevertheless, despite a massive drop in the number of entrants, it wasn't my week. In Week 3, I tried putting my recipe in verse form. Still no luck.

By Week 4, then, it was time to go all in. That my recipe was going to have strawberries was a given, but I was also going to saddle it with a frankly indecent number of tennis puns. Thus:

> *Let* me take *advantage* of this opportunity to *knock up* something with strawberries – surely you can't *fault* me there?! It'd be *ace* to *lob* in some rhubarb *pulp* too – a *mixed double* of classic British flavours. But *hold* on a sec – if you really want a *smash* hit of

> a drink, I'd *love* to add a little ginger and
> *serve* with a smile! (Trust me – folks will
> be making a *racket* about this juice for
> years!)

Fortunately, it was one of those weeks where nothing
succeeds like excess – helped by the fact that the drop-
off in entries had continued, and fewer than 350 people
had thrown their hat in the ring.

At this point, all that remained was to get a
babysitter, book train tickets, buy trousers and, oh, tell
my wife...

Procuring rail tickets at short notice is seldom cheap,
and this occasion was no exception. What I did not
expect was that the most economical way to arrive in
London would be to travel first-class. I was also not
expecting the coffee to be quite as dreadful as that
served in the under-class carriages, but there you go.

Fascinating as it is to see how the other half lives,
that brief insight dissolves into grimy dust the moment
you board whatever hot, stinking Tube train connects
you to Southfields.

On the plus side, the walk to the grounds is
straightforward and the conga line down Wimbledon
Park Road refreshingly genteel.

Before going any further, I must come clean about
my ticket kink: I love the physical experience of
slapping my ticket on the counter and swanning inside
ahead of the Johnny-come-hopefuls. It might sound like
mild schadenfreude, but it's actually far simpler: I just
dig on tangible credentials.

For this very reason, being on a guest list stresses
me right out. I daren't look behind me as I'm convinced
I'm being shadowed by some fat-pawed security gorilla
who's pegged me as a cheap ligger.

In reality, of course, no one ever bats an eyelid. The woman at Gate 5 handed me the grounds passes and funny little cardboard buttons, and relieved me of the weight upon my shoulders. Not the whole weight of course, as there was still the matter of locating the hospitality suite – but given the unambiguous guidance in my invitation (literally: it's just opposite Gate 5) how hard could that be?

In case you're unfamiliar with the grounds of the All England Croquet and Lawn Tennis Club, what's opposite Gate 5 is Centre Court itself. So, in the absence of any obvious signposting, we found a chap in an official blazer loitering outside Centre Court and begged directions. And what glorious directions they were – taking us right to the far end of the grounds where the various corporate partners had their marquees – major corporate partners like Jaguar and HSBC, but not Robinsons.

Three further members of staff later and we were exactly where we started – except this time, we noticed the wee notice directing guests to the Robinsons Suite.

It took just five minutes to start feeling sorry for those poor schmoes slumming it in the suburbs with Ralph Lauren. Inside, just a flight of stairs away from the action, it was air-conditioned and spacious; outside on the balcony, meanwhile, was pleasantly shaded with a birds-eye view of Joe Public and the impeccable flower arrangements. A more perfect spot to sip our first Pimms of the day I couldn't have imagined.

As we topped up our vim, two further fantastic things became clear: first, the guests in the room were all compers, so the atmosphere was one of genuine over-the-moon excitement; and second, the spectacle was set to exceed everyone's expectations, as the second men's semi was yet to be resolved. To this end, lunch was brought forward so we could watch two sets of Nadal v Djokovic.

It didn't take an expert to see that this was tennis of the highest calibre. These guys were so evenly matched that on any other day I'd have described the next couple of hours as epic. However, as the preceding semi ended 24 v 26 and lasted six and a half hours, the rivers of hyperbole were running dry.

Thanks to this unscheduled bonus, our afternoon tea was a bit of a frantic affair. On the one hand, I hope never to have to neck champagne at such a dangerous pace again; on the other, it's a risk I'm prepared to take.

Finally, then, it was time for the headline event.

The ins and outs of the match have inevitably been documented by writers far finer than I, so I'll forgo the details, suffice to say that we were really rooting for Serena, but sadly it was not to be. What we did witness, however, was the climax of a legend's year-long journey from intensive care to a grand-slam final, followed by one of the most wonderful examples of grace in defeat that anyone could hope to see.

Miss Williams didn't simply congratulate her opponent for winning her first title, but shared her pleasure in that moment, while praising her for being an incredible person and a really good friend.

As for being the 'super-human supermum' that the interviewer suggested she was, she replied, 'No, I'm just me and that's all I can be … I look forward to just continuing to be back out here and doing what I do best … It was such an amazing tournament for me. I was really happy to get this far … I can't be disappointed. I have so much to look forward to – I'm literally just getting started'.

The fact that one of the greatest professional success stories of all time doesn't take winning for granted is a massive takeaway, not just for athletes and sports fans, but for compers too. Like any seasoned comper, I have failed to win thousands of times. What's more, I have every intention of continuing to do so. Indeed, I similarly refuse to be disappointed when things don't go my way: if I'm looking back, it's not because I'm lingering on what might have been; it's because I'm enjoying past successes or learning from previous fails. Mostly, however, I'm looking forward, because I'm just getting started too.

Somewhat satisfyingly, the wisdom of Wimbledon did not end here either. As everyone trickled back into the hospitality lounge, the bartender leaned over to my comping buddy and whispered, 'We're closing the bar in ten minutes, so if I were you, I'd rack them up while you still can.'

For me, this is the best kind of advice as I can process it in a fraction of a millisecond, because, well, I'm just me and that's all I can be.

Xylophone

I have never won a xylophone.

You

For me, 2018 was great in so many ways. Beating my personal best was obviously awesome, as was winning a tote bag emblazoned with an oversized aubergine emoji, but more important was my growth as a comper. For example, I pulled off my first proper tie-break win; I made my first proper forays into purchase-necessary comping; and I made first contact with real-life compers!

Real-life compers?! The very idea! When I first started comping, I ploughed a lonely furrow. Ploughed it like a headless chicken, perhaps, but absolutely on my tod, if only because I was shy of barging in on other people's conversations or tagging strangers on social media comps.

Fortunately, compers tend to be a lovely bunch, and my wallflowering was not long tolerated. I might still be unclear about the ethics of tagging women I've never actually seen in competitions to win lingerie, but it's only a matter of time before someone puts me straight.

All the same, there was a time when the likelihood of ever being unable to hide behind my online persona was sufficiently remote as to be academic.

Then, of course, came my Wimbledon win, and with it (to use the official collective noun), a great big hospitality suite of bona fide, meat-based compers – just like me. This blew my mind.

I've never found social situations particularly easy, and the risk that I might have to respond to someone in real-time with no opportunity to hole up and craft my response with monk-like focus, made me extremely nervous. Fortunately, my wife was there to rescue me from social awkwardness and over-enthusiasm with the complimentary refreshments, while a brilliant comper I'd long admired took me under her wing, and assured me that over-enthusiasm with the complimentary refreshments was actually my moral duty, and, moreover, next time I should bring Tupperware and pack a little something for the journey home.

A shared win, of course, is a wonderful day out, and it's impossible not to have a good time. But what about a meet-up in everyday life – and one without free champagne at that?

Still good, as it happens. A pilot group of four Norwich compers convened towards the end of the year, and to the best of my knowledge, we all survived. Better still, plans are afoot for future, larger meetings, though whether they will be large enough for me to pick up where my wallflowering left off remains to be seen.

All this is just the warm-up, however. Before the end of 2019, I will be putting my panic attacks to one side in order to sit in a room full of 150 compers – a whole community of compers.

When I was new to comping, I found the concept of a comping community hard to grasp. After all, weren't we all in competition with one another? If Anna beats Betty to win the widget, why is Betty so happy for Anna – who she hasn't even met? For the newbie, alone and isolated, it's difficult to understand. That's why we take the red pill.

Betty knows she'll have another chance to win a widget. Indeed, Betty knows that there is no end to the widgets waiting to be won. But that's not half the story.

The truth is, there could be any number of reasons *why* Anna and Betty have become friends; what's more important is *how*.

As a born-digital comper, I can't imagine what comping was like before the days of social media, but I'm pretty sure I would have drifted out without it.

Much as it pains me to be thankful for Facebook, for example, I am.

True, there were forum-based communities, such as Loquax, before Facebook hooked itself into the world's veins. However, the Facebook interface is more friendly and intuitive, and as a result has really democratised things. As such, there are now all manner of comping-related forums, from the massive Lucky Learners group, to groups that specialise in sharing everything from local comps to winning notifications to prize-specific and entry-mechanic specific comps.

In short, if you want information, there are many places to get it. Or, to look at it another way, there are many places for compers to congregate. And as humans are social animals, they do exactly that.

So, it's good to talk.

It's also good to invest in those communities. Because what goes in gets paid back with interest.

Sure, you could lurk, hoovering up the intel. But then who's going to talk to you? Who's going to provide that extra set of eyes to look out for comps on your wishlist, or challenge you to comping bingo?

Who's going to check up on you when you disappear off the map? Who's going to mail you tinned wasabi for no reason other than to make you smile?

In other words, how are you going to make friends? Because that's what posting, commenting and chatting does for you.

Making friends isn't a bonus, or a nice-to-have. In our efforts to get to the bottom of what's eating our first-born, we identified that he is totally isolated within his year group. Watching your kid be lonely is hard enough, but when you learn that it's through friendships that we gain the peer-validation that is so fundamental to self-esteem, which in turn fuels our resilience, so much becomes clear. He's a ball of frustration, perpetually agitated, argumentative, always the victim, and despite his talents, has abysmal self-esteem. He has very poor emotional literacy, but given that he has so little opportunity to exercise his emotional articulacy during the day, that's hardly a surprise.

Making friends makes you grow as a person.

Likewise, making comping friends helps your comping persona to bloom.

Is your comping persona you, the whole you and nothing but the you? Of course not.

No one logs onto a comping forum to start a thread about their forthcoming MOT; neither do they comment on a promoter's competition posts to tell them how they ran out of leeks last night and are planning to pop down Aldi just after the school run.

Such information might create a more three-dimensional picture of the person behind the avatar, but it's hardly germane to the task in hand, ie comping.

What *is* germane is this: your passions. Yes, we all love Apple tech and holidays, but I'm talking about everyday passions.

One of my comping friends demands to be tagged whenever there's tea or peanut butter at stake; another has a standing order for cheese. Let's say your thing is socks. That being the case, I'm assuming you've already entered every last sock competition out there. Well, that's a start.

The next step is to tell all your comping buddies that that's what you've been up to. Share the comps with them – tell them just how much socks excite you! No – more than that! How you live for socks. How you breathe socks. How you would swap your first-born for a barrel of socks.

Start tagging your friends in other comps (Twitter is especially good for this), and nudge the conversation to – you've guessed it – socks. It doesn't matter if the comp is for biscuits or dishwasher tablets – steer the narrative to socks.

Why? Because if you're prepared to be the crazy sock lady, the next time your comping buddies see another sock giveaway, you'll be the first person they think of, and before you know it, you've got a dozen eyes out there, hunting down sock comps, and you can start banging on about the next thing – granola perhaps? Socks full of the stuff!

Zen

One day last week, as I decanted the final box of Maldon sea salt, an exquisite memory prevailed over me, and at once the monotony of the chore became indifferent to me – the travails of the day innocuous, the grind illusory. This new sensation had on me the effect which fortune has of filling me with a precious essence; or rather this essence was not in me, it was myself. I had ceased now to feel mediocre, accidental, mortal. Whence could it have come to me, this all-powerful joy? I was conscious that it was connected with the salt, but whence did it come? What did it signify? How could I seize upon and define it?

OK, let's not over-egg the pudding: I recently filled the salt pig with the final box from a set of three 250g 'limited edition' packets of Maldon sea salt I won a couple of years prior. Although the prize was one of the most modestly valued items I've ever won, its arrival sticks in my mind more than most. Partly that's because it turned up out of the blue, and partly it's because I remember remarking how mailing three-quarters of a kilo of salt cost three times what that salt was actually worth.

Mostly, however, the prize sticks in mind because salt is such an elemental part of our very existence: our bodies become chemically unbalanced without it, our muscles and nervous system cease to function and, well, I guess we die.

As it happens, I consume less salt than I'd like. That's not a conscious choice; rather, it's because, like many parents of small children, we cook without it and then fail to season our food as we're too absorbed in whatever argument we're having with the aforementioned beasts. That's why I seize moments to enjoy it as conspicuously as possible. I'm talking super fresh, crusty bread with creamy unsalted butter, a sprinkle of flaked sea salt and *no* interruptions.

I'll grant that as legacies go, inventing the salt sandwich is only slightly more impressive than the shoe umbrella, but that's missing the point: the important thing is to be mindful of how even the smallest of prizes can touch you on an absolutely fundamental level – in this case, the absorption of an essential daily mineral for somewhere in the region of 24 months – or as a more superstitious comper might say: two years' worth of lucky dust.

That lucky dust was actually the small tail of a much larger prize – a cute little Weber barbecue.

For the record, I hate cooking. My kitchen expertise extends to a full English (no beans), sandwiches, and washing up. I excel at washing up. My dish-washing game is up. My technique is fully academic Shaolin temple black-belt ninja Tokyo-stomping Godzilla Krypton Factor good. But you can't eat it.

At the same time, however, I love to grill. It's not just that there's something primal about it, or that my life zenithed when my first-born was ten weeks old and I barbecued for 20 days solid. There's also the fact that I love reconnecting with my prizes – in this case, the aforementioned Weber.

Mayday 2018 was the hottest day of the year, and while I was out basking in my mum's garden, I noticed myself enjoying a warm, if slightly unfamiliar, fuzzy feeling. It wasn't just the sun radiating positive vibes – although that always helps; the long overdue family reunion helped too. But what was really warming my cockles was watching the coals ash over as we prepared the first barbie of the season.

The process of setting up my Weber always starts with a smile as I recall how it was for some years the largest object I'd ever won, and how it arrived on the same day as the least physically imposing prize I've ever received: a font.

Truthfully, that font has had precious little impact on my life. Unlike, for example, the Jorg Gray watch I won from a 2015 Warner Bros promotion, which I was using to time the cooking that day, while sipping my prize lager from the preceding advent season, and wearing one of the brand-spanking shirts I won less than a fortnight prior.

And while I watched the children guzzle the fizzy drinks we'd fixed with the strawberry purée I'd also won over Christmas, I thought to myself: I'm so glad I decided to be lucky.

In the same vein, when I first started writing this, I was wearing a sweater I won a few Christmasses ago, having just boxed up the night's leftovers in the Happy Jackson pots I won that same year and packed away the football shirt I won during the last World Cup. This was after making my first-born stop reading his Roald Dahl book and put away his X-Men headphones, both of which I won in 2016, and washing up my wife's flask (won 2017), and before applying the fancy eye serum mentioned previously.

Am I a premier league comper? I doubt it. On the off-chance that I do somehow qualify for the top-flight, I'm very much a Huddersfield – standing under the armpits of giants.

Indeed, I'm in perpetual awe of the many fantastic – and more importantly – dedicated compers out there, whose drive to win the big-ticket prizes is plainly inspirational. People like Di Coke (https://superlucky.me/) and Nikki Hunter-Pike (https://glamandgeekymum.com/), for example, spring to mind – and not just because of their success, but also because of their community spirit.

Next to these guys, I'm a blatant also-ran. But that's also cool. Comping isn't a sprint race; if anything, it's a marathon. I've been in the game for around five years now, and despite a few episodes of mojo fatigue keeping me on the sidelines, the wins have slowly but surely stacked up, and my new-found 'luck' has manifestly embedded itself into my life. I have documented evidence that I'm a winner and I'm literally surrounded by my good fortune. On top of this, there's the awesome feeling I get now that so many friends are looking out for me – isn't that the money-can't-buy experience that everyone really wants?

The bottom line is that thanks to comping, I get the opportunity to feel good about myself every day – good enough to wind down the meds even.

Some might call my win rate unremarkable, but that's no bad thing. Unremarkable, means replicable. It means that anyone with half a mind to 'be lucky' can do just that. What's more, because when every prize is a happy moment made concrete, anyone who does choose to be lucky will soon find countless opportunities to celebrate success.

To be sure, this isn't exactly the kind of mindfulness that my wellbeing courses set out to teach. Nevertheless, by taking time to contemplate each episode of joy that I can literally hold in my hand each day, I'm starting to find my brain holding on to the cheer for longer. Or at least until it's time to collect the children from school anyway.

Further reading

Beesley, R. (2018) 'Overcoming the Odds: How I won
    £50,000 of prizes in three years', available at:
    https://www.amazon.co.uk/Overcoming-Odds-
    prizes-three-years-ebook/dp/B07HR2WXFR/.
Blue Chip (2018) 'Blue Chip and Plenty launch an
    INCREDIBLE promotion', 5 June, available at:
    https://wearebluechip.co.uk/blue-chip-and-plenty-
    launch-an-incredible-promotion/.
Britton, P. (2017) 'Why is there an 8ft sculpture of Jeremy
    Clarkson's head in this Salford garden?',
    Manchester Evening News, 20th February,
    available at: https://
    www.manchestereveningnews.co.uk/
    news/greater-manchester-news/8ft-sculpture-
    jeremy-clarksons-head-12630191.
Broeker, F. (2018) 'Get paid £20 an hour as a professional
    competition enterer', *Money Magpie*, 5 October,
    available at: https://www.moneymagpie.com/
    make-money/become-a-professional-competition-
    enterer.
Broeker, F. (2018) 'Become a professional McDonald's
    Monopoly player for £45/ph', *Money Magpie*, 24
    May, available at: https://www.moneymagpie.com/
    make-money/become-a-professional-mcdonalds-
    monopoly-player-for-45-ph.
Carr, R. (2017) 'Humiliating scam led to mum and
    daughter licking Poundworld staff's feet after fake
    phone call', Devon Live, 29 August, available at:
    https://www.devonlive.com/news/devon-
    news/humiliating-scam-led-mum-daughter-
    394060.
Caven, J. (2018) 'Armed man storms McDonalds and
    threatens staff, before leaving with box of
    Monopoly stickers', *Independent*, 3 May, available
    at: https://www.independent.co.uk/
    news/uk/crime/mcdonalds-monopoly-stickers-

mask-armed-west-london-police-latest-
a8334186.html.

Clear, J. (n.d.) 'Why facts don't change our minds',
available at: https://jamesclear.com/why-facts-
dont-change-minds.

Coke, D. (2015) 'SuperLucky Secrets: 100 tips for winning
competitions, contests and sweepstakes', available
at: https://www.amazon.co.uk/SuperLucky-
Secrets-competitions-contests-sweepstakes-
ebook/dp/B011QUY2HO/.

Cullinane, P. (2018) 'Will Ant and Dec super-fan miss out
on Florida holiday – despite having tattoo of duo?',
Stoke Sentinel, 21 March, available at:
https://www.stokesentinel.co.uk/news/stoke-on-
trent-news/saturday-night-takeaway-ant-dec-
1363960.

Ellis-Petersen, H. (2016) 'Boaty McBoatface wins poll to
name polar research vessel', *Guardian*, 17 April,
available at: https://www.theguardian.com/
environment/2016/apr/17/boaty-mcboatface-wins-
poll-to-name-polar-research-vessel.

Graham, C. (2016) 'Russian teen wins month in hotel with
pornstar in online competition', Telegraph, 25
February, available at: https://
www.telegraph.co.uk/news/newstopics/howaboutt
hat/12172724/Russian-teen-wins-month-in-hotel-
with-pornstar-in-online-competition.html.

International Olympic Committee (2017) 'Steven
Bradbury, Australia's last man standing',
available at: https://www.olympic.org/
news/steven-bradbury-australia-s-last-man-
standing.

Orwell, G. (1946) 'The Moon Under Water', *Evening
Standard*, 9 February, available at:
https://www.orwellfoundation.com/the-orwell-
foundation/orwell/essays-and-other-works/the-
moon-under-water/.

Richards, A. (2017) 'Iceland staff hid under tables and
"pretended to be vacuum cleaner" after mystery
hoax call', Mirror, 25 May, available at:

https://www.mirror.co.uk/news/uk-news/iceland-staff-hid-under-tables-10499196.